THE STATES AND THE NATION SERIES, of which this volume is a part, is designed to assist the American people in a serious look at the ideals they have espoused and the experiences they have undergone in the history of the nation. The content of every volume represents the scholarship, experience, and opinions of its author. The costs of writing and editing were met mainly by grants from the National Endowment for the Humanities, a federal agency. The project was administered by the American Association for State and Local History, a nonprofit learned society, working with an Editorial Board of distinguished editors, authors, and historians, whose names are listed below.

Colorado

A Bicentennial History

Marshall Sprague

W. W. Norton & Company, Inc.
New York

American Association for State and Local History
Nashville

Published and distributed by W. W. Norton & Co., Inc.
500 Fifth Avenue
New York, New York, 10036

Library of Congress Cataloguing-in-Publication Data
Sprague, Marshall.
    Colorado: a bicentennial history.

    (The States and the Nation series)
    Bibliography: p.
    Includes index.
    1. Colorado—History. I. Title. II. Series.
F776.S76   978.8   76–9800
ISBN 0–393–05599–X

Contents

Illustrations

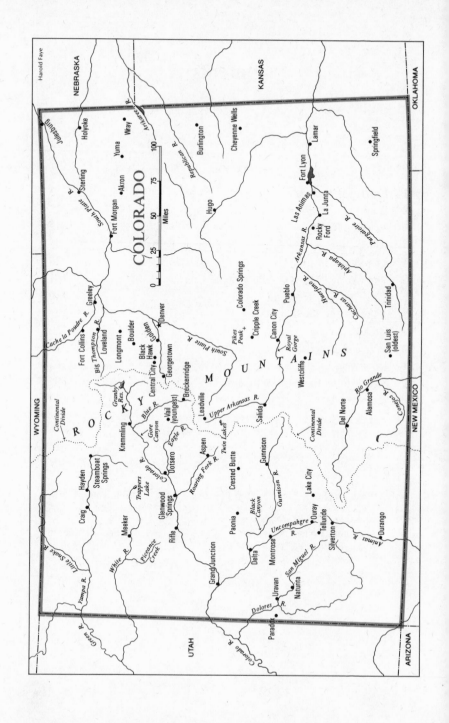

Invitation to the Reader

IN 1807, former President John Adams argued that a complete history of the American Revolution could not be written until the history of change in each state was known, because the principles of the Revolution were as various as the states that went through it. Two hundred years after the Declaration of Independence, the American nation has spread over a continent and beyond. The states have grown in number from thirteen to fifty. And democratic principles have been interpreted differently in every one of them.

We therefore invite you to consider that the history of your state may have more to do with the bicentennial review of the American Revolution than does the story of Bunker Hill or Valley Forge. The Revolution has continued as Americans extended liberty and democracy over a vast territory. John Adams was right: the states are part of that story, and the story is incomplete without an account of their diversity.

The Declaration of Independence stressed life, liberty, and the pursuit of happiness; accordingly, it shattered the notion of holding new territories in the subordinate status of colonies. The Northwest Ordinance of 1787 set forth a procedure for new states to enter the Union on an equal footing with the old. The Federal Constitution shortly confirmed this novel means of building a nation out of equal states. The step-by-step process through which territories have achieved self-government and national representation is among the most important of the Founding Fathers' legacies.

The method of state-making reconciled the ancient conflict between liberty and empire, resulting in what Thomas Jefferson called an empire for liberty. The system has worked and remains unaltered, despite enormous changes that have taken

vii

place in the nation. The country's extent and variety now sur-
pass anything the patriots of '76 could likely have imagined.
The United States has changed from an agrarian republic into a
highly industrial and urban democracy, from a fledgling nation
into a major world power. As Oliver Wendell Holmes remarked
in 1920, the creators of the nation could not have seen completely how it and its constitution and its states would develop.
Any meaningful review in the bicentennial era must consider
what the country has become, as well as what it was.

The new nation of equal states took as its motto *E Pluribus
Unum*—"out of many, one." But just as many peoples have
become Americans without complete loss of ethnic and cultural
identities, so have the states retained differences of character.
Some have been superficial, expressed in stereotyped images—
big, boastful Texas, "sophisticated" New York, "hillbilly"
Arkansas. Other differences have been more real, sometimes instructively, sometimes amusingly; democracy has embraced
Huey Long's Louisiana, bilingual New Mexico, unicameral Nebraska, and a Texas that once taxed fortunetellers and spawned
politicians called "Woodpecker Republicans" and "Skunk
Democrats." Some differences have been profound, as when
South Carolina secessionists led other states out of the Union in
opposition to abolitionists in Massachusetts and Ohio. The result was a bitter Civil War.

The Revolution's first shots may have sounded in Lexington
and Concord; but fights over what democracy should mean and
who should have independence have erupted from Pennsylvania's Gettysburg to the "Bleeding Kansas" of John Brown,
from the Alamo in Texas to the Indian battles at Montana's
Little Bighorn. Utah Mormons have known the strain of isolation; Hawaiians at Pearl Harbor, the terror of attack; Georgians
during Sherman's march, the sadness of defeat and devastation.
Each state's experience differs instructively; each adds under-
standing to the whole.

The purpose of this series of books is to make that kind of un-
derstanding accessible, in a way that will last in value far
beyond the bicentennial fireworks. The series offers a volume
on every state, plus the District of Columbia—fifty-one, in all.

Each book contains, besides the text, a view of the state through eyes other than the author's—a "photographer's essay," in which a skilled photographer presents his own personal perceptions of the state's contemporary flavor.

We have asked authors not for comprehensive chronicles, nor for research monographs or new data for scholars. Bibliographies and footnotes are minimal. We have asked each author for a summing up—interpretive, sensitive, thoughtful, individual, even personal—of what seems significant about his or her state's history. What distinguishes it? What has mattered about it, to its own people and to the rest of the nation? What has it come to now?

To interpret the states in all their variety, we have sought a variety of backgrounds in authors themselves and have encouraged variety in the approaches they take. They have in common only these things: historical knowledge, writing skill, and strong personal feelings about a particular state. Each has wide latitude for the use of the short space. And if each succeeds, it will be by offering you, in your capacity as a *citizen* of a state *and* of a nation, stimulating insights to test against your own.

James Morton Smith
General Editor

Colorado

1

Emerging Empire

*T*HE state of Colorado, its rolling plains barricaded by the Continental Divide and a jumble of Rocky Mountains of matchless height, width, and majesty, began to take shape when Napoleon doubled the size of the infant United States by selling to it everything he owned west of the Mississippi at a price of four cents an acre.

The year of this Louisiana Purchase was 1803. The president who approved the bargain was Thomas Jefferson. Half of what would become Colorado lay in a division of the Purchase that was called Unorganized Territory after 1821. The other half, south and west of the Arkansas—or was it Red?—River belonged to his Catholic Majesty, Charles IV of Spain. The boundary was in dispute.

It is useful to bear in mind this Spanish heritage. The word *colorado* is a Spanish adjective meaning "red" or "ruddy," which fits a common hue of the Colorado Rockies very well. Much of the future state was explored and claimed by the Spanish two centuries before the English colonists on the Eastern seaboard knew anything about it. The Spanish were not the first explorers and claimers. Various Indian peoples had been there for ages. At least as early as 1 A.D., the Basketmakers of the prehistoric Anasazi culture were living in shallow rock shelters

3

called pit houses in the Animas and La Plata River areas near the present city of Durango. They were succeeded after 700 A.D. by the Pueblo Indians of the same basic Anasazi culture living in cliff dwellings like those in present Mesa Verde National Park. All those beautiful place names in southern Colorado were bestowed by Indians of a later date and by Spanish priests. *Cochetopa* is an Indian word meaning "pass of the buffalo." The priests honored two of their Catholic saints by the designations of San Luis Valley and the San Juan Mountains. They applied *Sangre de Cristo* to both the lovely range and the pass across it. The name—meaning "blood of Christ"— referred to the deep-red glow that the priests observed flooding the crest at sunrise.

The region which is now Colorado was penetrated by Europeans not from the Mississippi but from the Rio Grande—from Santa Fe, the dusty little sun-baked capital of Spain's province of New Mexico, which was founded out there at the end of the world in 1610, and from the much older Pueblo Indian village of Taos near it. By 1700, Spanish traders in huge sombreros and long, clanking spurs were trailing mule trains over Raton Pass to Indian settlements near today's La Junta, Colorado. In 1719, Pedro de Villasur led a scouting party over Raton some five hundred miles across eastern Colorado to Platte River in present Nebraska, where most of the men were killed in an ambush by Pawnee Indians.

Colorado had its first prospectors in 1765—Juan Maria de Rivera and his Spaniards, who wandered into the Gunnison River country to scratch for gold that did not materialize. In the American birthday year of 1776, even as the rebels in Philadelphia were declaring themselves free from George III, the young Franciscan priests, Dominguez and Escalante, and eight friends of theirs from Santa Fe tramped through the sage plateaus and Ute Indian valleys of Colorado's western slope. In his diary of the trip, Escalante mentions that a black man—the first of countless blacks who would participate with the whites in developing Colorado—drowned in a flooding river. We still call the stream by Escalante's name for it, the Dolores—"River of Sorrows." Dominguez and Escalante got no farther west than Utah Lake, but theirs was an epic attempt to strengthen Spain's feeble grip on her remote northern empire by trying to find a way from New Mexico to Spanish California. Three years later, Governor Juan Bautista de Anza and a troop of soldiers, colonists, and Pueblo Indians, chased a troublesome band of Comanches northward out of San Luis Valley by way of Poncha Pass and on to the plains below Pikes Peak, killing many of them, including their leader Chief Cuerno Verde (Greenhorn), in a battle below present Greenhorn Mountain south of the Arkansas.

The question can be asked—why did the Spanish fail to push their settlements on the Rio Grande northward to lands in Colorado that were just as fertile? They had plenty of time—two centuries and more. One trouble was the lack of financial and military support by his Catholic Majesty in Madrid. Another was the archaic Spanish practice of forcing the native Pueblo Indians to do the work of developing farms and building adobe churches along the river. As a result, Spanish settlement stopped in the Taos area because there were no docile Pueblo Indians living in San Luis Valley beyond it. The valley was used only by the fierce plains Comanches and mountain Utes, nomadic horse Indians who prized their freedom to roam and refused to be held on some Spanish hacienda to plant corn and beans.

When President Jefferson bought that vast wilderness from Napoleon in 1803, the problem arose whether its boundary in the Spanish southwest was the Arkansas River or the next stream south of its drainage, Red River. Since no American of record had got within a thousand miles of the Colorado Rockies, the army sent a handful of soldiers from St. Louis to see what Jefferson had bought out that way—to search for the source of both the Arkansas and the Red while finding out what they could about Spain's border defenses north of Santa Fe and Raton Pass without actually trespassing on Spanish property.

The sixteen soldiers were led by Captain Zebulon Montgomery Pike, an able young captain from New Jersey who had been fighting Indians and exploring the Mississippi Valley for a decade. Pike's ignorance of the new American West was total. He imagined it to be similar to the trans-Appalachian East in its distances, altitudes, climate, and rivers. He and his party left St. Louis in June of 1806 wearing summer clothes since they expected to be back home by October. But they were still creeping west over the high Colorado plain on a chill November 15 when they first saw, from the Arkansas near present Las Animas, the Front Range of the Rockies rising ahead like a low cloud.

The isolated landmark that would be called Pikes Peak in honor of its "discoverer" (the Spanish and Indians had known it for a century and more) sprawled, snowcapped, to the northwest. To the southwest the shivering soldiers could see the slate-gray Spanish Peaks of the Sangre de Cristo Range, with a dip to the left of them (Raton Pass) and another on the right (Sangre de Cristo Pass into San Luis Valley). They guessed that Pikes Peak was about as high as one of those four-thousand-foot ridges in western Pennsylvania, and perhaps a day's march away. But a day's march did not bring them perceptibly closer. Two weeks passed before they reached the forested base of the big mountain and tried to get through the snow of the foothills in a fruitless effort to climb it. Pike put its altitude a bit high—18,582 feet above sea level. The actual height is 14,110 feet.

What followed was one of the bravest and most foolhardy episodes in the history of American exploration. Rather than be sensible and hurry back to the familiar East, Pike and his men gazed at the great ranges stretching into blue mists beyond Pikes Peak and succumbed to their mystery and challenge. They had to try to conquer them, impelled by the ancient conflict between humankind and earth. They made winter clothes and shoes out of buffalo and beaver skins and deer hide, stocked up on venison, and ascended the rushing blue Arkansas past the site of present Canon City.

They had no guide. Blocked by the granite walls of the Royal Gorge, they moved northwest up Currant Creek into South Park, one of those four huge, mountain-ringed basins that give the Colorado Rockies their aura of immensity. The horses played out in the wind-tortured desolation of the park's nine-thousand-foot altitude. For many weeks thereafter the men struggled along on foot to survive the deep freeze that comes to Colorado's highlands in winter. They spent Christmas day dreaming of the comforts of St. Louis as they huddled around a pitch-pine bonfire below present Leadville and the headwaters of the Arkansas. A battalion of summits towered above them, including Mount Elbert and Mount Massive, which would be designated later as highest and second highest of fifty-odd Colorado peaks rising above fourteen thousand feet. Pike spotted a forlorn western evening grosbeak and called it a Carolina paroquet, following his habit of trying to make East fit West.

Through January the wretched men staved off starvation and their own mutinous tendencies as they trudged through the deep snow of Wet Mountain Valley south of the Royal Gorge. They had located the source streams of the Arkansas. Now they had to find Red River. Near the site of present Westcliffe, below the spectacular Crestone Needles of the Sangre de Cristo Range, the temperature sank one night to fifty-three degrees below zero. Two soldiers woke up in the morning with their feet so frozen that they became crippled for life.

All sixteen of them would have perished if the weather had not moderated to springlike temperatures in February—a common Colorado phenomenon. A Ute trail led them over the Sangre de Cristos at Medano Pass (*medano* means "dune" in Spanish), bringing them to the eerie Great Sand Dunes and the sage flats of San Luis Valley. With soaring spirits they decided that the sparkling river running through the valley had to be the Red. But it was Spain's Rio Grande. Decades later the source of the Red would be found hundreds of miles to the southeast in West Texas. They built a rest camp near a warm spring on Conejos River, a branch of the Rio Grande. After some days, a squad of Spanish soldiers, tipped off by the Utes, appeared at the camp and arrested the Americans for trespassing in New Spain. They hauled them downstream to Santa Fe to be questioned as spies, and escorted them seven hundred miles farther south to jail in Chihuahua. This was routine behavior for Spanish officials in New Mexico. They had a pathological fear of foreigners and foreign invasion and had banned trade with the Mississippi settlements for a century. Pike was not released to American authorities at Natchitoches in Orleans Territory until July 1807. Some of his men were more than a year getting home.

The plains and mountains of Colorado dropped out of the American mind during the War of 1812 but reappeared in 1819 when the United States and Spain agreed to put the southwest boundary between New Mexico and Unorganized Territory on the Arkansas River to its source and then due north. Some months later, the new nation moved across the Mississippi politically, at last, when Missouri became the twenty-fourth state with a bombastic St. Louisan Thomas Hart Benton as its first senator. This major leap toward Colorado occurred in 1821, just as the people of Mexico won their independence from Spain. The Mexicans dropped the old Spanish trade ban, and a dynamic Missourian William Becknell led a pack train from St. Louis to the Arkansas and over Raton Pass and sold his wares in the Mexican provincial capital of Sante Fe for seven times their cost.

Becknell used three wagons on his next trip west, in the spring of 1822. He avoided the steep Raton Pass trail by pioneering a desert route away from the Arkansas near its great bend and along Cimarron River. Both routes would become standard as the Santa Fe Trail from St. Louis—the Cimarron Cut-Off for wheeled caravans with enough employees to fend off raids by Comanche Indians, and the so-called "mountain division" over Raton Pass for pack trains and small emigrant parties.

During the next twenty years, the Santa Fe Trail lured from Missouri to the future Colorado a few hundred young fur traders and trappers who found there a new American dream—a climb-and-conquer way of life that satisfied their yearning for adventure, for self-reliance, for absolute freedom. Some of these mountain men—Kit Carson, Jim Bridger, Tom Fitzpatrick (nicknamed "Broken Hand"), Lucien Maxwell—would become national heroes. Their methods of surviving in the wilds, borrowed from the Indians, would help the gold-rush people later to endure that strange environment with its mild and raging weather, utter dryness and heavy rain and snow, tonic air too thin for easy breathing, and light too bright and clear for eyes used to the misty vistas of the lowlands. And always both mountain men and gold seekers had to cope with the future state's drag of gravity, produced by the highest mean altitude in the nation—nearly seven thousand feet above sea level.

While the fur boom of the 1830s lasted, these free spirits came to know every Indian trail and tribe in the Colorado Rockies as they combed the wilderness for beaver and trade. They explored all the high parks by way of Ute Pass around Pikes Peak and Sangre de Cristo Pass west of the Spanish Peaks. They followed the ancient trail from San Luis Valley over Cochetopa Pass, a low Continental Divide crossing connecting Pacific and Atlantic waters. Cochetopa brought them to Gunnison River, rising in the Saguache Range and guarded on the north by the red Elk Mountains. On the banks of the Gunnison near present Delta, a Frenchman from Quebec Antoine Robidoux built a trading post to serve the Utes of the Uncompahgre Valley.

The capital of this high empire was Bent's Fort, a post on the Upper Arkansas built 1828–1832 by two St. Louis natives William and Charles Bent and their partner, a Missouri-born French Creole Ceran St. Vrain. Bent's Fort was a medieval city in effect—its warehouses, living quarters, saloon, and billiard hall enclosed by high adobe walls with corner bastions and loopholes for guns and cannon. Scattered for miles around it were hundreds of buffalo-hide tepees. They belonged to Cheyenne and Arapahoe Indians, several thousand of whom used as their hunting ground the Colorado plains east of the Front Range from the Arkansas to the North Platte.

All of this Unorganized Territory west of Missouri had no government whatever. The Bent brothers were the law, acting as judges and sheriffs in keeping peace among the Indians and travelers on the Sante Fe Trail. In 1838, the Bents built a second trading post, Fort St. Vrain, in the rich South Platte valley downstream from the present site of Denver. The two posts were connected by road and allied with Fort Laramie on the North Platte, which was owned by the big Eastern monopoly the American Fur Company.

A large conspiracy becomes part of the story here—a plot that would change, in a few turbulent years, not just the face of the American West but of the nation and the world. The future state of Colorado was a pivot point in plans conceived by that perennial senator from Missouri Thomas Hart Benton, who had campaigned for years to enlarge the United States by still another million square miles, as Thomas Jefferson had done in his deal with Napoleon. When the fur boom collapsed in the late 1830s, Benton's plans were complete—to make the nation a continental power by pushing a thousand miles beyond the crest of the Rockies to the Pacific at the expense of the Mexicans and the Indians, and also of the British, who had been sharing Oregon with the United States since 1819 in a joint-occupancy arrangement. The senator believed that after the Americans captured the west coast, they would soon control the fabled trade of the Orient.

Benton's strategy, to be justified soon by the ringing phrase, Manifest Destiny, seemed much too rash to succeed. But cosmic forces, pure happenstance, even dumb luck, conspired during that incredible decade of the 1840s to bring it off. There were problems. The Mexicans were alarmed in 1836 because Americans under Sam Houston had seized their province of Texas. To make things worse, Houston had moved the boundary of his Texas Republic, in theory at least, west to the Rio Grande and north beyond its source in the high Rockies— thereby claiming a stovepipe of Mexican land thrusting up through Colorado and containing the sites of pleasant western-slope towns such as present Gunnison and Steamboat Springs.

Another problem was the apathy of Americans generally to western expansion—apathy originating in 1820 when Major Stephen H. Long led an army expedition up the South Platte to the Colorado Front Range. Long's men were scientists and artists, not adventurers. They had none of the derring-do of Pike's soldiers in 1806. The major spotted the thrilling twin towers of Longs Peak from a distance, named the peak after himself, and moved on. His botanist, Dr. Edwin James, picnicked in the Garden of the Gods near present Colorado Springs and drank of the bubbling waters of Manitou. He took notes on rock wrens and dusky grouse and climbed Pikes Peak, starting a forest fire in the process. Long named the peak after Dr. James, but the name didn't stick. The major's explorers made feeble attempts to penetrate the Colorado mountains up South Platte Canyon, Ute Pass, and the Royal Gorge, and called it a day, complaining that a stingy government had failed to supply proper equipment for such dangerous work. They returned east by way of Raton Pass and the Canadian branch of the Arkansas, which they mistook for Red River.

The Long expedition had other negative results. In his official report, Long labeled the high plains of eastern Colorado "the great American desert" and added in part:

> In regard to this extensive section of the country we do not hesitate in giving the opinion that it is almost wholly unfit for cultivation, and of course uninhabitable by a people depending upon agriculture for their subsistence. . . . The whole of this region seems peculiarly adapted as a range for buffalos, wild goats, and other wild game, incalculable multitudes of which find ample pasture and subsistence upon it. The region, however, viewed as a frontier, may prove of infinite importance to the United States, inasmuch as it is calculated to serve as a barrier to prevent too great an extension of our population westward. . . .[1]

Americans of that day tended to judge subsistence in terms of the crop farming that they knew in the East. Most of them did not ask themselves how a region could be a desert and still have "ample pasturage" to feed "incalculable multitudes" of buffalo. Long's pessimism, extended by public opinion to the West as a whole, was very bad for Benton's conspiracy two decades later. It gave strong support to the antiexpansionist wing in Congress. To counteract it, Benton arranged with the War Department to send forth an expedition which would combine military reconnaissance with promotion to make the wilderness more attractive to Americans. To head this public-relations group, the senator selected his son-in-law Lieutenant John Charles Frémont of the corps of topographical engineers.

It was an inspired choice. The mercurial Frémont had the kind of irrepressible optimism, the self-confidence, and daring that matched the senator's grandiose objectives. He was a small, agile, humorless youngster, and tense, like a clock too tightly wound. He had a horror of the commonplace, the obvious, the dull. He liked to do things his way, which was usually the hard, melodramatic way—a tendency inherited from his mother, a Virginia belle named Anne Whiting. In her teens, Anne married

1. Percy S. Fritz, *Colorado* (New York: Prentice-Hall, 1941), p. 80.

a sixty-five-year-old major and then, on a casual impulse, ran off with a charming young Frenchman Charles Frémont who had just been dismissed from his teaching job in Richmond for living with a woman to whom he was not married. Charles did not get around to marrying Anne either during their years of rambling about the South, even after John Charles was born in 1813.

But illegitimate birth was no handicap for the precocious son of the two fashionable delinquents. As a student in South Carolina, he won, by his brilliance at law and science, an influential sponsor, President Van Buren's secretary of war, Joel Poinsett, for whom the crimson plant was named. Poinsett put Frémont to mapping the Iowa country with the topographical engineers in 1838, which brought him to the attention of the redoubtable Benton and his beautiful daughter Jessie. When the seventeen-year-old Jessie and the twenty-eight-year-old Frémont met at a musicale in Georgetown, they gazed at each other while lightning flashed, or so Jessie put it, and thunder clapped. It was that kind of romance. Benton opposed the union of his child to a minor officer of scandalous background, so the lovers eloped to a Washington hotel and were wed there on October 19, 1841.

The senator forgave them and got his Manifest Destiny under way the following spring by sending Frémont to map the American part of the Oregon Trail from the Missouri River at Westport up the North Platte and Sweetwater to the Continental Divide at South Pass. The purpose of the trek was to encourage the migration of American farmers to Oregon, which would overwhelm the sprinkling of Britishers there and hasten sole possession of that region by the United States. Frémont did not care for the bleak Wyoming stretch of the Oregon Trail. He found it a killer for horses and oxen, infested with hostile Indians, scenically depressing, and much too roundabout to suit the military plans of his father-in-law for seizing California.

The lieutenant determined to find better, shorter, more exciting routes—through the granite core of the Colorado Rockies instead of around it. Though the conquest of California was his prime concern, he yearned to test himself in the highlands as Captain Pike had done, to be the first to study Colorado's wild-life and geology, to see how and where those primary rivers with their immense strategic potential got started—the two Plattes and the Arkansas flowing to the Mississippi; the Rio Grande to the Gulf of Mexico; the Grand, which the mountain men had found joining Green River in present Utah to form the Colorado on its way to Grand Canyon and the Gulf of California.

And so Frémont took a new route out of Westport in the spring of 1843. He headed directly for Fort St. Vrain and Longs Peak by following the Kansas and Republican rivers, which par-alleled the Oregon Trail some one hundred miles to the south. He was sure that he would avoid Captain Pike's misadventures. Modern technology was on his side in the form of the latest in waterproof tents and rifles, an eighteen-foot India rubber boat, emergency rations, chronometers, sextants, barometers, tele-scopes, compasses. A curious item of his equipage was a wheeled howitzer shooting twelve-pound balls, which he bor-rowed on the sly from the army's commander in St. Louis, Col-onel Stephen Watts Kearny. The lieutenant was not supposed to take along anything as martial as a ton of howitzer. His mission was ostensibly scientific—to continue mapping the emigrant Oregon Trail beyond South Pass to the mouth of the Columbia. But, he told Kearny, he might have to detour a bit on Mexican soil. In that case the cannon might serve as a substitute for a passport.

It could be presumed that Frémont had his bride Jessie in mind when he chose his personnel. Jessie would write from his notes the report for Congress of both his first and second ex-peditions. She deserved to have material as colorful and as romantic as their own love affair. Frémont's thirty-nine com-panions in 1843 did not look like staid topographical engineers. Most of them were French Canadians from St. Louis and French

Creoles from New Orleans, wild men in fringed buckskin, of the kind who had roamed the Rockies through the fur-trade period and had given French names to bits of Colorado—Cache la Poudre ("hide the powder") River near Fort St. Vrain, for example, and Fontaine Qui Bouille (Fountain Creek today), derived from the bubbling springs of Manitou. Frémont's head guide was Tom Fitzpatrick, who had helped to discover South Pass in 1824. His hunter was Lucien Maxwell, an Illinois native who was about to marry a fifteen-year-old heiress named Luz Beaubien from the New Mexican village of Taos. Mlle. Beaubien's French father had just received vast land grants lying on both the Mexican and Colorado-to-be sides of Raton Pass from Manuel Armijo, the governor of New Mexico. Armijo made these grants to encourage settlement in that part of his Mexican province as a measure of border defense against American pressure from north of the pass.

Some miles out of Westport, Frémont found himself obliged to accept a tagalong as an act of kindness, a tall, lean young lawyer from Independence, Missouri, William Gilpin, whom he had known for some months as an ardent supporter of Senator Benton. Gilpin told Frémont that he had sold his law books for $60 and had borrowed $100 to buy a woebegone steed named Old Flash on which to ride to Oregon, where he hoped to show the pioneer settlers how to organize a territorial government. Though Frémont was reluctant to believe that there could be another young man as unusual as himself, this distinguished-looking, twenty-seven-year-old deadhead made him wonder. Gilpin did not tell lies exactly. He just stretched the truth a bit for dramatic effect—claiming, for instance, that he was born on the battlefield at Brandywine, Pennsylvania, though his actual birthplace was in the family home on Brandywine Creek, Delaware. He had attended school in England and at the University of Pennsylvania, and went to West Point for a term as a protegé of President Andrew Jackson. He fought the Seminoles in Florida and left the army to become editor of *The Missouri*

Argus in St. Louis before settling in Independence as a lawyer.

As the Frémont expedition set out for the Colorado Rockies, its leader discovered that his guest did not converse. He orated, and his joy in what he had to orate was so great that it was impossible to interrupt him. Frémont found that Gilpin was far ahead even of Senator Benton in his enthusiasm for the West, based on information which he claimed to have received from the great mountain men.

Novel notions bubbled up from his mind like soup boiling over. He had learned, he said, from European friends such as the Marquis de Lafayette and Alexis de Tocqueville—he was fond of dropping names—that gold as a medium of exchange was in desperately short supply because of the growth of world trade since the American Revolution. Its production heretofore had been a monopoly of kings and tyrants. But now, he declared, American democracy made it possible for anyone to go hunting for it where it was certain to be found—in the core rocks of the mountain west. And this gold boom could cause a transcontinental railroad to be built, linking Boston and St. Louis with the Pacific coast. From the Pacific, the rails could push on to Moscow and London by means of a bridge over the shallows of Bering Strait. The highest Rockies, Gilpin concluded, his eyes closed in a prophet's rapture, were located along the healthy, stimulating "isothermal zodiac"—the 40th parallel of latitude—where all progressive people lived. These particular Rockies would provide an ideal site for a city along the international railroads.

Frémont had time to hear only a few of young Gilpin's prophecies. He could not dream, of course, that this voluble soothsayer was destined to become the first governor of the Territory of Colorado. Mostly the lieutenant was occupied with the thrills, pains, and novelty of the Great Plains—scorching heat by day and chill nights, Indian alarms, flopping magpies, rattlers, burrowing owls, buffalo so numerous at times that they stretched solidly to the horizon. A month of travel brought the expedition into the Frenchman Creek antelope-and-coyote country of eastern Colorado where, half a century later, the dry-farming towns of Holyoke and Haxtun would rise. In describing the approach to the site of present Sterling, Jessie Frémont, as her husband's ghost-writer, had reactions similar to those of today's Denver-bound tourists on that same route in early summer:

> On the afternoon of the 30th of June we found ourselves overlooking a broad and misty valley where about ten miles distant, and 1,000 feet below us, the South Fork of the Platte was rolling magnificently along, swollen with the waters of the melting snows. It was in strong and refreshing contrast with the parched country from which we had just issued, and when, at night, the broad expanse of water grew indistinct, it almost seemed that we had pitched our tents on the shore of the sea. Travelling along up the valley . . . in the afternoon of July 1 we caught a far and uncertain view of a faint blue mass in the west as the sun sank behind it; and from our camp in the morning, at the mouth of Bijou (Creek), Long's Peak and the neighboring mountains stood out into the sky, grand and luminously white, covered to their bases with glittering snow.[2]

Frémont's men found plenty of that splendid Mexican beverage called Taos lightning—because of its rapid striking power—with which to celebrate Independence Day when they reached Fort St. Vrain on July 4, 1843. Three days later, needing more mules, Frémont rode south with his German cartographer, Charles Preuss, bound for the small trading post at the junction of Fountain Creek and the Arkansas. Lucien Maxwell had been sent ahead to Taos earlier for the mules, but he was overdue, and Frémont assumed that Luz Beaubien, his betrothed, was keeping him home. Moving up the South Platte in the shadow of the Front Range, the two tourists admired the striking sandstone formation that would become Denver's Red Rocks Park

2. Donald Jackson and Mary Lee Spence, eds., *The Expeditions of John Charles Frémont,* 1 vol. to date (Urbana, Ill.: University of Illinois Press, 1970), 1:435.

and crossed Black Forest Divide, beflowered with purple lupine and fairy trumpet, to Pikes Peak. Guided by the Edwin James report of 1820, they found the bubbling springs of Manitou, which Preuss praised as equal to the famed seltzer-water of the Rhenish Duchy of Nassau. No mules were to be had at the Arkansas post—future site of the steel city of Pueblo. But Frémont was delighted to find Christopher (Kit) Carson passing by on his way to Bent's Fort.

Carson, aged thirty-four, had been Frémont's hunter on the 1842 trek to South Pass. He was already a legend as a tireless mountain man with a phenomenal memory of western trails, rivers, and ranges. Carson agreed to buy mules at Bent's Fort and bring them to Fort St. Vrain, then to guide one Frémont party in search of better military routes west while Tom Fitzpatrick took the official expedition due north to the "uninteresting"—Frémont's word—Oregon Trail. The two groups would meet on Snake River later and continue together to Oregon. On July 26, 1843, Carson led the small Frémont group northwest through the Front Range along the north fork of the Cache la Poudre, with the Mummy and Never Summer peaks rising southward and the Medicine Bows to the west. Kit's obscure Indian trail brought them over Dead Man Hill Divide and out of Colorado to the spacious Laramie River valley in what would be southern Wyoming.

A year passed before Frémont's adventurers saw those highest Rockies again—a year of hardship and peril as they trailed to Oregon and southward. Most of their mules perished, and the stolen howitzer was abandoned during a desperate winter crossing of the Sierras from the Great Basin of present Nevada into Mexico's California. Of the expedition's original thirty-nine, only two dozen worn-out men made it, in the spring of 1844, from Southern California across the Mojave Desert and on to Antoine Robidoux's Fort Uintah in eastern Utah. They took the Spanish Trail, the Colorado part of which had been pioneered by Dominguez and Escalante in 1776—the trail used by rustlers driving mules from California to Santa Fe.

Two days of rest at Fort Uintah restored the travelers wonderfully. They were a happy, if tattered, group on June 7, 1844, as they slid their mules—Kit Carson leading, Frémont next—off Diamond Mountain and down Crouse Canyon into the multicolored Green River valley of Brown's Hole in what would be the extreme northwest corner of Colorado. The weather was crisp and sunny as they explored a bit of Lodore Canyon, gorged on antelope and bighorn sheep, and picked up fossil evidence of ancient days when Colorado was the tropical home of dinosaurs and crocodiles. They trailed eastward through the sage along the pink rimrock of the Little Snake River, and over the Continental Divide in the Battle Lake Pass area to North Platte River.

For three cloudless days they ascended that diminishing stream south through the scenic glory of North Park, shooting a few elk for food and amusing themselves by trying to lasso a grizzly bear. It was, Frémont noted,

> . . . a beautiful valley of thirty miles diameter, walled in all around with snowy mountains. . . . We fell into a broad and excellent trail, made by buffalo, where a wagon would pass with ease, and in the course of the morning, we crossed the summit of the Rocky Mountains through a pass which was one of the most beautiful we had ever seen.[3]

That was Muddy Pass (8,772 feet above sea level), a sort of branch of Rabbit Ears Pass, beloved these days by skiers crossing to Steamboat Springs and the Yampa River valley. Muddy Pass brought them to Grand River (today's Colorado) and the modern dude-ranch community of Middle Park. From there on June 22 they crossed the Continental Divide to South Park over what homesick gold seekers later would call Hoosier Pass

---

3. Jackson and Spence, *Expeditions of Frémont,* 1:712–713.

(11,598 feet above sea level). In the thin air atop Hoosier, Carl Preuss and Kit Carson made a map of those fundamental waterways, the Rio Grande, two Plattes, Arkansas, and Grand, all of which began as cheerful trout streams trickling down from this tremendous snowcapped cluster of Colorado ranges, most of which were visible from where the cartographers sat. Ten days later, using Pike's Indian route across South Park, the travelers reached the Arkansas and Bent's Fort. Another month of trailing east on the Smoky Hill River trail put them back in Westport and St. Louis, completing five thousand miles of exploration.

In the Colorado high country, the crack of a rifle can start an avalanche. Jessie Benton Frémont's vivid story of her husband's expeditions in 1842 and 1843–1844 had the effect of an avalanche on the course of Manifest Destiny when her report was published in August of 1845. Frémont was not around when it appeared. He was leading his third expedition of sixty men through the Colorado Rockies by way of the Arkansas and Tennessee Pass, bound for the Pacific coast and military action.

Millions of Americans became expansionists as they thrilled to Jessie's version of what had happened to Frémont and Kit Carson and Tom Fitzpatrick and the rest in Colorado, in Oregon, in California—lands glamorous in themselves and made all the more so by Jessie's exuberant hyperbole. Brigham Young and his Mormons, suffering unbearable persecution in Illinois, studied her account of Frémont's trip to Great Salt Lake and began plans that led to their western Kingdom of Deseret in 1847 and to the creation of Utah Territory three years later. The American migration to Columbia River became a flood, causing Great Britain to give up her Oregon claims south of the 49th parallel.

The appearance of the Frémont report coincided with the furious reaction of the Mexican government to the annexation of Texas, which gave President Polk the excuse he needed to declare war on that impoverished and martially feeble country. On July 22, 1847, Frémont's friend General Stephen Watts Kearny and an army of 1,700 men arrived at Bent's Fort. The soldiers built a road over Raton Pass and seized Santa Fe on August 18 without a shot being fired. Four months later Kearny added California to his conquest of the New Mexican Southwest.

The peace treaty of Guadalupe Hidalgo, an event ranking with the Declaration of Independence and the Louisiana Purchase in the evolution of the United States, was signed February 2, 1848. It brought success to Senator Benton's conspiracy beyond his wildest dreams. But even as the Mexican and American commissioners were signing the treaty, something of special importance to the future of Colorado was taking place a thousand miles farther west—in California. This happening was the discovery by a sawmill mechanic named James Marshall of pure gold in the sands of a tributary of the American River.

2

Boom Days

$\mathcal{T}$HE swift expansion of the nation to the Pacific combined with the swarming of gold seekers to California and of Mormons to Utah shattered the peace of the Colorado empire that the Bents had ruled from their two posts on the Arkansas and the South Platte. The resident Indians felt the change most—several thousand Utes scattered through the lower valleys of the highest Rockies, and the more numerous Cheyennes and Arapahoes on the bordering plains below Longs Peak.

When the California gold rush began, the Cheyennes and Arapahoes were disturbed by the commotion along the Oregon Trail. The hordes of travelers and their animals ruined grazing and hunting along the North Platte, and spread disease and alcoholism among the Indian natives. To alleviate these evils, Tom Fitzpatrick, who had become an Indian Bureau agent, called a meeting of nine Plains tribes near Fort Laramie in September 1851.

Fitzpatrick told some thousands of these Indians that each tribe was a nation in its own right, but the highest authority was the Great White Father in Washington who worked for everybody, white, red, and black. Then he presented a Senate treaty, which twenty-one chiefs signed. By the treaty the government agreed to give the nine tribes fifty thousand dollars worth of trade goods annually for the next fifty years in exchange for the right to build roads and army forts within the nine nations. In setting boundaries for each nation, the treaty assigned to the Cheyennes and Arapahoes the land lying between the North Platte and Arkansas rivers—mainly the plains of eastern Colorado and what is now southern Wyoming.

The Colorado Utes did not attend the Fitzpatrick assembly. They were spared Oregon Trail problems because of their isolation. If anything, their supply of wild game increased as elk, deer, antelope, and bear moved into their Rockies to get out of the paths of westward migration. There were six bands of these short, stocky Utes who behaved like Plains Indians but were related linguistically to the Aztecs of Old Mexico. The six bands had little tribal unity and they were only mildly martial, lacking the fierceness of the Comanches and Kiowas of eastern New Mexico and the Cheyennes of the Colorado plains. Still, they could be dangerous. They continued to claim the San Luis Valley as their hunting ground after it became American in 1848, and they were quick to attack New Mexican emigrants arriving from the Santa Fe region. As a result, the U. S. Army built, in 1852, near the west foot of Sangre de Cristo Pass, the first military base in Colorado, Fort Massachusetts (relocated and named Fort Garland in 1858) to protect these new American citizens. Among them were six New Mexican families sent by Charles Beaubien to colonize the northern half—called Trinchera—of the million-acre Sangre de Cristo grant, which Governor Armijo had approved in 1843. The six families founded the pioneer Colorado town of San Luis in 1851. Three years later another group from New Mexico founded Conejos on the Continental Divide side of the valley.

These San Luis Valley New Mexicans were ancestors of the largest ethnic minority in today's Colorado—some two hundred thousand of them. Through the past century they have been described by various names—Spanish-Americans, Mexican-Americans, ''Spanish surnamed,'' Hispanos—winding up fi-

nally in the popular designation of 1976, Chicanos. Like the
state's predominant Anglos—"Anglos" meaning the white population of whatever European origin—they are a complicated
blend of many ethnic groups. The blend, predominantly Indian
with Spanish overtones, has evolved through the centuries of
their residence in Mexico and New Mexico after the Spanish
conquest of Mexico in 1521. The blend has resulted in a distinctive and fascinating culture, which has resisted change and has
clung to old traditions, the Catholic religion mixed with Indian
beliefs, and the Spanish language. Life in Colorado today owes
a great deal to the color, artistry, and emotional depth of this
Chicano culture in contrast to the materialistic and relatively
drab culture of the Anglos.

   The hostility of the Utes to the northward advance of the New
Mexicans had applied also to the Forty-Niners, California
bound, who had found it wise to pass around their mountains instead of through them. The unpredictable weather was another
good reason for avoiding the Colorado Rockies.

   Travelers recalled how the Oregon missionary Dr. Marcus
Whitman nearly lost his life during a winter crossing in 1842 of
Cochetopa Pass on his way from Fort Hall in present Idaho to
Santa Fe. Six years later, a bitter John Charles Frémont, tempo-
rarily out of the army for doing things too much his own way in
California, came to San Luis Valley to find a railroad passage
through the mountains for his father-in-law, Thomas Hart Benton. Frémont's party of thirty-five was caught in a blizzard
while searching for Cochetopa Pass. Eleven men died of starvation or freezing, and a few of the dead were eaten by survivors.
In 1853, Captain John W. Gunnison, also hunting a rail route
by way of Cochetopa, had endless grief trying to pass through
the impassable Black Canyon of the Gunnison and across the
rugged Cerro Summit to the Uncompahgre valley. Some weeks
later, Gunnison met his death in Utah when he was shot full of
arrows by Paiute Indians. His euphonious name came to be

applied to town, county, and river in a Colorado mountain setting of special beauty.

The vast Unorganized Territory of the Louisiana Purchase did
not begin to break up into pieces until 1850, when the Forty-
Niners won statehood for California and the Mormons persuaded Congress to create the Territory of Utah, bounded in the
Colorado Rockies partly by the Continental Divide. At the same
time Texas gave up its Colorado stovepipe, and the Territory of
New Mexico was formed with a north boundary along the Arkansas as in Louisiana Purchase days. New Mexico's east
boundary was put at the 103rd meridian.

Then came the tragic struggle over whether slavery should be
permitted west of Missouri. Kansas Territory was formed in
1854 with the slavery question left up to the Kansans, causing a
rush of settlers pro and con to squat on lands beyond the Missouri. The north boundary of Kansas Territory was at the fortieth parallel running west to the Continental Divide. That line
put the sites of present Boulder and Greeley, Colorado, and
most of the South Platte valley in the new Nebraska Territory.
The south boundary of Kansas Territory ran along the thirty-
seventh parallel until it hit New Mexico's east boundary, where
it swung north a degree to the Arkansas at present Las Animas,
Colorado, and west again to the divide. This swing north left in
New Mexico Territory the historically Spanish region between
Raton Pass and Bent's Fort.

One of the counties in Kansas Territory set up in 1855 was
called Arapahoe, starting at the 103rd meridian just barely in
sight of Pikes Peak and running on west to Utah Territory at the
crest of the Rockies. Since this huge wilderness was nearly
empty of white settlers and belonged by treaty to the Cheyennes
and Arapahoes, no officials were appointed to run it.

But events conspired to populate Arapahoe County. The gold
of California sparked a nationwide business expansion, which

led millions of otherwise normal people to dream of becoming filthy rich overnight by finding gold or by speculation in gold stocks back East. Financial recklessness ensued, causing the panic of 1857. Before the panic ended, a number of gold seekers rode up the Arkansas from the Missouri and into the wilds of Arapahoe County to escape their creditors and the fratricide of "bleeding Kansas." Some of them joined men from Georgia in the summer of 1858 and found bits of gold in sands near the junction of Cherry Creek and the South Platte (downtown Denver today) not far from the boundary of Nebraska Territory. They sent glowing tales back home about fortunes to be picked up "at Pikes Peak." Though that massive pile was eighty miles south of their placer diggings, it was the best landmark to guide newcomers. As a result, the Pikes Peak label came to be applied to the entire Front Range region from the Arkansas northward two hundred miles to Longs Peak and the Cache la Poudre.

One of these pioneer parties of 1858, numbering forty-nine people from Lawrence, Kansas, came to achieve a very special distinction. The party included two wives on a rugged adventure, which was regarded widely as suitable for males only. One of these wives, a twenty-year-old bride named Julia Archibald Holmes, made her position clear at the start by wearing what she called her "reform dress"—a calico dress to the knee, and pants called "bloomers," named for Amelia Bloomer, the militant editor of the woman's rights publication, *The Lily*. When told that the men thought she looked queer in this costume, Julia replied, "I cannot afford to dress to please their taste. I couldn't positively enjoy a moment's happiness with long skirts on to confine me to the wagon." [1] While the Lawrence party was camped at the foot of Pikes Peak, Julia learned that no woman, and very few men, had managed to reach the summit. The

1. Julia Archibald Holmes, *A Bloomer Girl on Pikes Peak—1858* (Denver: Western History Department, 1949), pp. 16–17.

challenge to be first of her sex was irresistible. She made it easily to the top on August 5, 1858, with her husband and two other men.

News of Julia's feat spread far and wide and was thrilling to American women everywhere. In retrospect, historians have found in it a sharp reminder that women in the West, as everywhere else, have always performed as well as men—women pioneering, suffering, challenging, creating, adapting, enduring. They have performed well even though their roles have been underplayed because of the custom, persistent until recent decades, of assigning to men alone most positions of leadership. It would be interesting to know just how many of the male heroes described in this Colorado story owe their triumphs to the wisdom and drive and courage of Colorado women directing their lives from behind the scenes.

The effect of the tales about Pikes Peak in 1858 was like fireworks on the Fourth of July—each burst more spectacular than the last. Soon the whole nation was gasping with wonder over the new El Dorado. Pikes Peak was only seven hundred miles from the Missouri—a fortnight's journey compared to three or four months of travel that the Forty-Niners had endured to reach California. Any Missouri farm boy, eyes shining with visions of freedom from poverty, could get to Pikes Peak with his mule, sack of flour, coffee pot, and slab of bacon. Eastern presses poured out guidebooks full of nonsense. The trails west filled with "Pikes Peak or Bust" young people, mounted and in wagons, buggies, and stagecoaches, or on foot pushing wheelbarrows. There was even a sail cart that worked for half a mile. Merchant caravans carried machinery, furniture, saloon equipment, and everything else needed in a mining camp.

The surface (placer) gold of Cherry Creek played out quickly, but the prospectors plunged deep into the mountains that winter, spurred by the same mystic challenge of altitude—the urge to see and conquer—that had inspired Pike and Frémont. Here in these unexplored ranges, folding westward one after another, the Continental Divide came closest to the eastern plains. Agreement was general that the granite spine of the divide was where the gold was. A rich placer strike was made on a branch of Clear Creek near the site of what would be Idaho Springs. And then a gold-bearing quartz vein was found, which was bound to extend into its mountain for miles. The success of this Gregory Gulch bonanza led to the founding of Central City.

Some fifty thousand people hurried to the Pikes Peak region during the following summer of 1859. Most of them were the usual American-melting-pot mix—young farmers of English and Irish extraction from Kansas and Iowa, Scotch-Irish from the Kentucky hills, Scotch and Welsh and Germans and Italians from Pennsylvania. There were many blacks—some of them slaves with their masters from Tennessee and Texas, some free men from the eastern states. "Aunt Clara" Brown opened a laundry in Central City and won celebrity both as the first black woman there and as the only nurse in Gilpin County. Barney Ford, who had been a slave in Virginia, came to Denver and went on across the Continental Divide to strike it rich at Breckenridge and to be elected to the territorial legislature.

These eager argonauts filled the highlands with their frenzy as they crawled up every gulch and over the divide into South Park, into the Arkansas Valley below Frémont's crossing of 1845, which they named Tennessee Pass, and over the divide to Pacific waters, to Middle Park, and the canyons of the Colorado River. The drama and beauty of the Rockies enthralled some of them, and they had a rapt audience—marmots and ptarmigan above timberline, soaring ravens staring down on them in sullen amazement. These prospectors brought business along the belt of their swarming—crude road construction, rest stations with feed for mules, blacksmith shops, tent saloons with faro tables, lean-to taverns—primitive havens which evolved into log towns like Tarryall and Fairplay on South Platte drainage, Breckenridge on the Blue River branch of the Colorado, and Oro City on the Arkansas.

Traces of law and order appeared in the shape of two villages on opposite banks of Cherry Creek. One was called Auraria, after a gold camp in Georgia. The other was St. Charles, recalling King Charles III of Spain who had owned Cherry Creek in Father Escalante's day, though its modern claimants chose that name with St. Charles, Missouri, in mind. As winter approached in 1858, General William Larimer arrived with authority from officials of Kansas Territory to give government to Arapahoe County. Larimer found St. Charles reduced to a population of one armed guard. Legend has it that he distracted the guard with a bottle of bourbon. While the guard was consuming the gift, the general and his aides took possession of St. Charles and renamed it Denver. General James W. Denver, a Virginian, served briefly as governor of Kansas Territory before sinking out of history in contrast to his municipal namesake, which he did not manage to visit until 1874.

The Pikes Peakers yearned for more government than County Commissioner Larimer could provide. During 1859, volunteers set up dozens of mining districts in the foothills with officers to record mining claims. Crime was punished by people's courts. Farmers squatting on plots along the streams registered their land with claim clubs. These informal institutions, pending government sanction, were patterned on those which had worked in California, and in New England two centuries before that. Some pioneers were aware that the region had been assigned by treaty to the Cheyennes and Araphoes in 1851, and were prompted to send agents to the legislature in Kansas and to Congress to have these Indian claims extinguished.

But in 1859 Kansas was a battlefield, the Civil War was brewing, and politicians had no time for the Pikes Peakers. To meet the impasse, a group of Denver residents met in the fall and created their own appendage of the United States—called Jefferson Territory by some, Jefferson State by others. It had its own government, following specifications drawn from the Northwest Ordinance of 1787 for admitting new parts of the public domain into the Union. But Jefferson Territory fizzled out before the summer of 1860, partly because of its unpopular poll tax. Its name was resented also, since Thomas Jefferson had been a slaveholding Democrat and most Pikes Peakers were Abraham Lincoln Republicans.

Agents for the majority of settlers got busy in Washington to urge Congress to approve their own version of a territory under a gamut of names such as the Indian "Yampa," the Spanish "Colorado" and "San Juan," and the amorous "Lula" (some miner's sweetheart). "Colorado" won out, and the whole matter was resolved by the rush of eastern events. Lincoln was elected president in November 1860. Kansas, with its present boundaries, was admitted as a free state. Secession of seven Southern states cleared Congress of anti-Colorado Democrats. The Republicans in Washington were eager now to please those influential owners of world-famous gold mines by creating Colorado Territory. That occurred by presidential proclamation on February 28, 1861.

The Pikes Peakers and their friends in Congress wasted no time enlarging the territory by stealing everything in sight. They acquired a strip of western Kansas sixty miles wide. From Utah Territory of the Mormons they took the Colorado Plateau west of the Continental Divide, which contained what is now Dinosaur National Monument and the prehistoric cliff dwellings of Mesa Verde National Park. From Nebraska Territory they snatched the richest part of South Platte valley and the future Rocky Mountain National Park below Longs Peak. They got all of New Mexico north of Raton Pass including the fertile farmlands of San Luis Valley and those along Huerfano River below the Spanish Peaks. These farmlands had special value. They lay within Governor Armijo's vast grants of the 1840s, which the U. S. Senate had agreed to honor in its treaty with Mexico. The agreement made the grants private land, open to legal purchase from the grantees, whereas the rest of the Pikes Peak region was in the public domain—federal land, which could not be acquired with clear titles until Indian claims were quieted and government surveys completed.

The Colorado Territory of 1861 was the same huge rectangle that the state of Colorado is now—nearly four hundred miles from east to west, three hundred from north to south. That came to a total of 66,718,000 acres. The Pikes Peakers created it, propelled by faith, greed, ambition, and zest for achieving the impossible. Few of them were serious thinkers, but some had gifts of leadership and foresight. There was, for example, William M. Byers, aged twenty-seven, a small dynamo with a flashing eye for pretty women and a mind abrasive enough to sharpen knives on. Byers hurried with a handpress from Omaha to Cherry Creek in April 1859, and began printing *The Rocky Mountain News*. For two decades thereafter his inflammatory editorials would blast away at "murderous, thieving Indians" and "idiot Democrats." Quieter paragraphs would promote his credo that Colorado's future lay in farming, manufacturing, scenery, and climate—not gold.

Though William Gilpin was not a Cherry Creek pioneer, he was a most effective booster working out of his home in Independence, Missouri. Much had happened to him since he headed for Oregon on Old Flash in 1843. After serving as a major in the Mexican War and fighting Comanches on the Santa Fe Trail, he returned to Independence to combine his law practice with real estate ventures and opposition to slavery.

But he spent most of his time spreading news about the wonders of the West. As his oratory improved, he grew handsomer and more impressive. His lanky six-foot frame filled out to nearly one hundred and fifty pounds. Throughout the Missouri Valley spellbound audiences came to regard him as a modern Demosthenes whose stately rhetoric lifted them above the day's pettiness and into the wisdom of the ages. The absurdity of some of his ideas was submerged by the tidal wave of his idealism. People were thrilled when he rose on tiptoe to castigate Major Long's report on the "great American desert." Western farmers, he declared, were blessed by crop yields richer than those of the Vale of Kashmir or the Holy Land. The westerners were the healthiest of men because of the tonic climate—mild winters, cool summers, and perennial sunshine.

He had embellished his dream of a railroad running by way of South Pass and Bering Strait to Moscow and London. To achieve global harmony—what he called "the immortal fire of civilization"—branch lines would be built up to it from Shanghai and Bombay, Cairo and Rome and Mexico City, so that all nations could share in this rail-induced prosperity of the favored "isothermal zodiac." But, Gilpin would conclude, there was a threat to his western Utopia. The Kansas–Nebraska Act of 1854 had encouraged slave-owning Democrats to hope that they could win the West and its golden treasures in the course of the impending War Between the States. Passage of this evil act, he said, had caused ex-Senator Benton to die of a broken heart. Gilpin himself had quit the Democrats and joined the Republican party even though he had been threatened with hanging in 1860 when he had cast, in Independence, the sole vote for Lincoln out of a total vote of 1,200.

Gilpin had voted for Lincoln as much by design as by idealism. He observed that the Pikes Peakers were about to get their Colorado Territory, which meant that President-elect Lincoln must be looking for a governor, preferably from a slave state like Missouri. He was sure of his strength in the North. So Gilpin appealed to Republican leaders in St. Louis, and things began to move. He had competition, a Dr. John Evans of Chicago who had platted a town, which he called Oreapolis, at the mouth of the Platte River, as a rival to Omaha. In this venture, which died in the panic of 1857, Evans had the help of a young Nebraska politician Samuel Elbert. Gilpin counted Evans out because he was from Republican Illinois where Lincoln needed no support. And Gilpin was, of course, better qualified, having risked his life riding to Oregon and back on the bony spine of

Old Flash whereas the effete Evans had never been west of Oreapolis.

Word came early in February 1861 that Lincoln wanted Colonel Gilpin along as a bodyguard on his train trip from Springfield to Washington, and in the White House through the inauguration. The Colorado candidate must have guarded the president well. Lincoln gave him the territorial governorship just before the Civil War began at Fort Sumter. On a crisp evening in May, Gilpin stood in dignified triumph on the lamplit balcony of the Tremont House in Denver overlooking Cherry Creek. Cannon boomed a welcome and, William Byers reported, "Denver's fairest maidens beamed" and wondered if this hazel-eyed bachelor of forty-five years could be plucked out of celibacy. (He couldn't. Gilpin resisted marrying for thirteen more years.) Colorado's first governor gave a grandiloquent speech about "the plateau of America"—narrowed now to the Colorado Rockies—"up which civilization will ascend to plant the sacred fires over its expanse and shine upon the world with renewed refulgence." Byers thought that the speech was good, if a bit long. His comment: "Colonel Gilpin is a very peculiar man." [2]

The Governor discovered that his government was a shadow regime, consisting for most of that summer only of himself, a U. S. marshal, and a secretary, Lewis Ledyard Weld. The Colorado capitol consisted of three small rooms above a Larimer Street harness shop. The legislature could not decide where and when to meet, or how many counties to create. There was no money in the treasury—which was Gilpin's wallet—because Congress had failed to appropriate any.

But what worried Gilpin most was lack of troops to defend the Central City gold mines. All the regulars had been called

2. Robert L. Perkin, *The First Hundred Years* (New York: Doubleday and Company, 1959), pp. 233–234.

east, except a handful at Fort Garland in San Luis Valley and at Fort Wise down the Arkansas. Rebel flags had been raised in Denver, and there were rumors that Confederates in the area were joining the Plains Indians to attack the town.

When Gilpin learned from people in Santa Fe that a Rebel force was forming in Texas under an ex-U. S. Army general Henry H. Sibley, he called the Pikes Peak region to arms. He may have exaggerated the danger, but he knew what was involved better than anyone else. He had battled Plains Indians. He had fought Mexicans along the road between Texas and Raton Pass—the ancient El Camino Real of the Spanish conquest. He knew that Sibley was a first-class officer, a West Pointer like himself. Sibley had been in charge of building Fort Union south of Raton Pass as the supply center for New Mexico's army posts. It was obvious to Gilpin that Sibley planned to capture Fort Union, which would give him all the military supplies he would need to seize the Denver region.

If Sibley took Denver and controlled the Santa Fe Trail and Oregon Trail, California was bound to fall to the Rebels. That thought gave Gilpin, the geopolitician, bad dreams in which he watched a jubilant Confederate envoy in London signing papers with the Chancellor of the Exchequer for huge loans, with the rich gold mines of Central City as security. The loans would pay for a great Rebel navy to drive Union ships from the Seven Seas and insure the delivery of Southern cotton to the mills of England.

Gilpin's call to arms was received with enthusiasm, resulting in the First Regiment of Colorado Volunteers, nicknamed "Gilpin's Lambs." The force consisted of 1,342 young miners, bartenders, lawyers, preachers, con men, shoe clerks, pimps, faro dealers, actors, and mule skinners. They received some slight training at a barracks on the South Platte near Denver, Camp Weld. One of their instructors was a three-hundred-pound giant, as bearded and oracular as Moses, the Reverend John M. Chivington, who had been serving the region as presiding elder of the Methodist Church. Having no territorial funds, the governor issued scrip on the U. S. Treasury worth $375,000 to buy guns and equipment and to pay for building Camp Weld. He had no authority to issue such scrip on his own, but he had seen Frémont do it in 1843, and he believed that he was saving the Union.

The merchants of Denver were happy to accept the scrip for supplies that summer, though their joy turned to rage in the fall when the U. S. Treasury refused to redeem the scrip that they had sent in. As the city sank into financial chaos, Gilpin took the long trail east to ask the Treasury to settle up with the merchants and to pay arrears on his own salary. His pleas failed. President Lincoln, absorbed in General Grant's campaign, had no time to study Gilpin's case, though he delayed until March 18, 1862, before removing him from the governorship.

Great irony here. As Lincoln made his decision, Gilpin's Lambs were tramping through a blizzard across Raton Pass to Fort Union and on south to block Sibley's regulars camped in Glorieta Pass short of Santa Fe, which they had just taken. On March 28, the confident Texans, their red state flag flying, advanced with cannon booming and grapeshot rattling on the weary Lambs crouched in an arroyo near Pigeon's Ranch. After two hours of combat, the Lambs had to retreat, leaving behind fifty dead and sixty-five injured.

The Texans had won a tremendous victory. Before them was the wide-open road to Denver. Or was it open? As Sibley prepared to continue north, word came to him that a bull-voiced preacher named Major Chivington and four hundred and thirty Lambs had dropped off the cliffs of Apache Canyon to capture his rear guard and set fire to his supply train—half a million dollars worth of vital ammunition, saddles, food, clothes, medicine, maps, wagons. As the supplies burned, the Lambs worked in relays shooting down six hundred spare horses and mules, the blood of which made a red creek flowing down the canyon.

That ended the Civil War in the West. Without arms or food, Sibley had no choice but to flee south—to try to get his men back to Texas before soldiers from the New Mexican forts could join the Lambs and hunt them down.

Back in Denver, Gilpin showed no bitterness over his removal from office as he welcomed the second governor of Colorado Territory in a brief ceremony at the Tremont House on May 16. Most of the applause went to "the Hero of Glorieta," Major John M. Chivington, who planned to run for Congress. The new governor, John Evans, got a spatter. William Gilpin got none.

John Evans was forty-eight years old when he reached Denver to take over as head of the territory, superintendent of Indian affairs, and commander-in-chief of militia. He was a blocky, slow-speaking man, solemn as a pontiff and careful to maintain his dignity as the most eminent Methodist in the middle west, and one of the wealthiest. He was born a Quaker in Ohio, got his medical degree in Cincinnati, and practiced for some years as an obstetrician in Indiana. He quit the Quakers and joined the Methodist Church because of its greater discipline and the solidarity of its members in matters spiritual and material. In 1846 he founded the Indiana Hospital for the Insane and invented a sort of mechanical hand with eleven-inch steel fingers for extracting babies during their birth. He never understood why the mothers were not enamored of the device.

After moving to Chicago in 1848, he gave up medicine for what really interested him—the pursuit of wealth and of power through business and politics. He dabbled in the latter while building a railroad from Chicago to Fort Wayne and founding Northwestern University and its town of Evanston, Illinois. In 1860 he coached his protegé Sam Elbert when the latter worked for Lincoln as a Nebraska delegate at the Republican national convention. Thereafter, Evans put in a bid for the governorship of Nebraska Territory or of Colorado. He felt that either of them would put him in line for his heart's desire, the U. S. Senate, since these territories were expected to achieve statehood soon. But President Lincoln could only offer Washington Territory—too far away. When Evans heard of Gilpin's scrip problems, he went after Lincoln again. This time he got the Colorado job.

Evans was a generous contributor to the Methodist Church and its educational projects. He was compassionate, after attending to first things first—wealth, power, political advancement. As a business administrator he was extraordinarily gifted. But as the chief executive of a vast untamed wilderness he had limitations. He was not a rugged pioneer type like Gilpin or Frémont. He had a distaste for any outdoors at all. He went fishing in Illinois once, got bitten by mosquitos, and was seldom seen again away from the inside of his home or office, except to hurry from one to the other.

Upon arriving in Denver, Evans found people leaving the Pikes Peak region in droves because of the money pinch brought on by Gilpin's depreciated scrip and because the gold boom was waning. The placers had played out and lode miners were having trouble with their gold veins as their shaft holes deepened. Near the surface the veins gave up their gold because the rock enclosing them was softened by erosion. Lower in the shaft, the gold resisted separation by any known process. The new governor restored some confidence by issuing optimistic statements on the economy and on the imminence of statehood—statements that he hoped would help him later when he would need the support of the legislature to put him in the Senate.

Evans was at home with these economic and political matters. But his big problem was the Indians, whose stubborn refusal to give up their savage ways and behave like white men baffled him completely. He knew that Tom Fitzpatrick's treaty of 1851 with the Plains tribes had turned out to be a sham, that none of its terms had been lived up to by the U. S. government. Many thousands of whites had dispossessed the Cheyennes and Arapahoes of the entire Pikes Peak region, which had been guaranteed them by the U. S. Senate. This injustice, Evans felt, had been corrected in 1861 when the Indian Bureau persuaded four chiefs to sign a new treaty at Fort Wise (Fort Lyon after 1862) down on the Arkansas. By its terms, the four chiefs exchanged the Cheyenne–Arapahoe lands of the 1851 treaty for five million acres bounded by the Arkansas on the south and by Sand Creek on the northeast. It was a huge chunk of high plains containing what is now the richest irrigated farmland of the Arkansas Valley between present Fowler and Lamar, with Fort Lyon in the middle.

But it was just a bleak and arid prairie in 1861. Here the members of the two tribes were ordered by the Indian Bureau to give up hunting buffalo for subsistence, as they had been doing since time out of mind, and learn instead how to farm on forty-acre plots. Many of the Cheyennes and Arapahoes did move to the Arkansas reservation to draw moldy rations—when they were available at all—from the Fort Lyon agency until somebody arrived from Washington to show them how to plow and build a house. But many remained nomads, explaining that they had to hunt or starve because the agency officials stole their annuities. They added that the four chiefs had no right to sign a treaty binding them.

Residents in Denver who knew something about Indians tried to explain to Evans why the Cheyennes and Arapahoes could not become farmers overnight—why their lives were dedicated to survival in a boundless environment, why they loved their hard way of living and found fulfillment and pride in it. The governor was sympathetic but insisted that these savages could not continue to block Christian progress by their extravagant and inefficient use of land. His opinion had the strong support of his fellow Methodist John A. Chivington, who had just been placed in charge of the Pikes Peak military district by the U. S. Army's commander in Leavenworth, General S. R. Curtis. Colonel Chivington argued that the promotion of progress was the governorship's top responsibility and God's will, even if the intransigeance of the savages forced the whites to destroy them, including their children. As Chivington pointed out, "Nits make lice." [3]

Chivington was a comfort to Evans through 1862 and 1863 as conflict increased between the Pikes Peakers and the Indians roaming illegally—in Evans's opinion, at least—over their old hunting grounds. The colonel's cavalry matched raid for raid, pillage for pillage, rape for rape, and sometimes a bit more. At Chivington's request, Evans bombarded the War Department with telegrams for funds to recruit more men to meet a rumored uprising of all the Plains Indians. Then word came in mid-June 1864 that four Arapahoes had stopped at the Van Wormer ranch twenty-five miles southeast of Denver and had murdered the tenant, Nathan Hungate, his wife, Ellen, and their two small daughters, Florence, six, and Laura, three. The mutilated bodies were found stuffed in a well. The governor did not feel it politic to intervene when Van Wormer carted the four corpses to Larimer Street and put them on display for anyone with the stomach to look at them.

Thereafter horror mounted in the Denver area as stories of Indian atrocities circulated. Food prices rose with the disruption of supply trains and mail service along the South Platte. In August Chivington got an order from the War Department to raise a regiment of one-hundred-day soldiers, the Third Colorado Cavalry. The governor issued a proclamation authorizing all citizens to "kill and destroy" hostile Indians on sight. He did not explain how to distinguish "hostiles" from "friendlies." He advised the "friendlies" to go to their reservation on the Arkansas so that they would not be shot at inadvertently. In late September a conference was held at Camp Weld, Evans and Chivington on one side, seven Indian chiefs on the other. It was a collision of frustrations, and it came to nothing. Chivington produced a telegram from General Curtis instructing him not to make peace

3. Perkin, *First Hundred Years,* p. 269.

"till the Indians suffer more." Evans expressed doubt about the sincerity of the chiefs and construed the general's telegram as relieving his office of authority in the crisis.[4]

After that conference the Cheyenne chief, Black Kettle, returned to the Arkansas reservation, which was his impression of what the governor had asked him to do. During October he collected several hundred Cheyennes and Arapahoes in families and installed them for the winter in a prairie village of tepees on Sand Creek forty miles northeast of the Fort Lyon agency. Over his tepee, the chief raised an American flag with a white flag beneath it to show that this was a village of "friendlies." At this point, Governor Evans packed up his wife and children and left Denver for a two-month visit to Washington.

The rest of the Sand Creek tragedy, told and retold in a thousand variations, occurred a fortnight later. At sunrise on a clear, cold November 29, 1864, Colonel Chivington and his Third Colorado Cavalry of nine hundred mounted men topped a ridge and saw on a bend of Sand Creek the many tepees of Black Kettle's village with Old Glory flying above them. The soldiers had ridden all night from Fort Lyon, nibbling on maggoty hardtack. They were miserably cold, unkempt, resentful, and near exhaustion, but sustained by Chivington's promise that they would be heroes like Gilpin's Lambs because they were about to wipe out this vile nest of murdering savages and end Colorado's Indian troubles forever.

A few Indians sighted the troops and made for their nearby herd of some six hundred horses. Chivington ordered the soldiers forward, shooting. Artillerymen on a bluff manned their four twelve-pound howitzers. As the tepees began to shrivel and collapse under cannon fire, men, women, and children, disheveled and bewildered, poured out, some with guns and bows and arrows, some with hands raised in surrender. The Indians ran toward the creek bank for protection, but the space between

4. Perkin, *First Hundred Years*, p. 208, 268.

the village and the bank was soon covered with bodies, dead and dying. Throughout the morning the one-sided carnage continued as the soldiers cleared Sand Creek for two or three miles of its defenders and completed the destruction of the village.

According to the testimony of witnesses later before two congressional committees, a madness seemed to possess some of the soldiers as they took to scalping fallen bodies, male and female, cutting off fingers, breasts, genitals for souvenirs, raping dead squaws in relays, using toddling children for target practice. By 4 P.M. the horror had ended—the village a flat litter, the flag purloined, the area gruesome with blood and torn corpses. Black Kettle was among those who escaped northward. There were no other survivors. Chivington allowed no prisoners to be taken. He forbade burial. The Third Colorado Cavalry simply rode away, leaving the dead to the coyotes and vultures.

The Third Colorado lost eight men killed, some of them in their own crossfire, and forty wounded. A "credible" estimate put the Indian dead at "something under two hundred." Two-thirds of the bodies counted later were women and children.[5]

5. Perkin, *First Hundred Years,* p. 272.

3

Marking Time

$\mathcal{T}$HE debate over what came to be called the Sand Creek Massacre erupted into a national as well as a Colorado political issue—the beginning of widespread concern for the plight of Indians in the West. It drove Chivington into exile and brought the removal of John Evans from the governorship by President Andrew Johnson in August 1865. Chivington had strong support in the territory at first, but sentiment turned against him when Captain Silas S. Soule was murdered on Larimer Street shortly after testifying against him in a Denver inquiry.

Chivington's boast that he had broken the will of the "savages" did not pan out. He merely increased the frustration of the two tribes and added to it the desire for revenge of all the Plains Indians from New Mexico to Canada. While the debate raged as to whether Black Kettle's village was a hideout for criminals or a haven for innocent families under federal protection, the Cheyennes and Arapahoes began a campaign to drive the whites from their ancient hunting grounds. As a result, the fear of Plains Indians lasted more than two years—until veterans of the Civil War returned to their army posts and forced removal of the two tribes to reservations in Indian Territory by terms of the Medicine Lodge Creek Treaty of October 1867. Much of the Indian devastation occurred along the Platte River trail in the northeast corner of Colorado. The warriors had a special triumph in February 1865 when they destroyed the town of Julesburg. This infamous stopover on the stage road to Denver had been headquarters for a clutch of white bandits, led by Jules Beni, who often covered their crimes by posing as Plains Indians.

Many people blamed John Evans as much as Chivington for Sand Creek, which was unjust. The governor was overburdened with insoluble problems during that Civil War period when no help came to him from Washington. The criticism pained him deeply. But he would not be deterred from the ambitions that had brought him to the wilds, and he had the comfort of his wealth and an attractive wife Margaret sixteen years his junior. By Margaret he had two toddling sons and, by his late first wife, a daughter Josephine, who pleased him by marrying Sam Elbert. Sam had become the governor's closest friend—a blood relative in effect. Until Josephine died of tuberculosis in 1868, Sam occupied a cottage in the Evans yard. Thereafter, he lived with the Evanses a good deal of the time.

Other events besides Sand Creek put Coloradans to marking time during the middle 1860s. Much had been expected of President Lincoln's Homestead Act of 1862 for getting the public domain into private ownership. But farmers had to pay claim fees and have these "free" one-hundred-and-sixty-acre tracts surveyed before deeds could be issued to them. Many Colorado surveyors of the General Land Office were incompetent and corrupt. Speculators acquired more land than the Homestead Act allowed by hiring people to claim homesteads and then buying them out. The platting of townships was a very slow process. The surveys of only a few along the Front Range were completed in the 1860s, and most of these had to be corrected later because corners were often marked by ephemeral blazes on trees or movable stones or even magpie nests.

The first townships in the Denver area were marked in 1861, following the plan devised in 1784 by a Continental Congress committee under Thomas Jefferson. A township was, and is, six miles square, consisting of thirty-six sections of 640 acres each. The east-west dimension of a western township is called a range, indicating how far it is in six-mile segments from the "sixth principal meridian," a longitudinal line just west of Abilene, Kansas. The Colorado township has a second number, a "tier," revealing its distance north or south of the "base line"—which is the fortieth parallel where Baseline Road in Boulder is now. In 1861 Denver was (and still is) located in a township described as "range 68 west"—408 miles west of the sixth principal meridian in Kansas—and "tier three south"—or eighteen miles south of that base line which serves as a street in Boulder.

Because of the increasing difficulty of removing gold from its ore, dozens of the camps that had boomed in 1860 were almost ghost towns by 1865. Disappointed miners on Blue River and the Upper Arkansas and in South Park thought of returning to the comfort and dull security of their homes back East but found themselves held by the appeal of their giddy environment, the spaciousness, the violence and serenity of the climate, the brightness of stars, and the gorgeous sunups. The hangers-on believed that their luck would turn, maybe tomorrow. Horace Tabor was typical of this irrational optimism—a Vermonter in his mid-thirties who mortgaged his Kansas homestead in 1859 to climb the beanstalk of hope with his wife Augusta and small son Maxcy. The trio crossed the plains to Denver and moved on to Colorado City at Pikes Peak, to Oro City in California Gulch near the head of the Arkansas, and finally over that frightening Mosquito Pass (at 13,188 feet still the highest road in North America) to a camp tucked like a bird's nest in a cleft under Mount Bross. Tabor christened the camp Buckskin Joe while serving as postmaster there before moving his family back to have another go at California Gulch.

Tabor was an engaging human being of average size and

mind and looks, gregarious, outgoing, moderately hardworking, honest as the falling rain. He found time to play poker, to dabble in county politics, to organize volunteer fire departments. Augusta was thin and small, smelling of starch and Calvinism. Hers was not a loving nature. She lacked sex appeal, preferring balanced budgets to the techniques of romance. But she was incredibly industrious, capable, and loyal. Though Horace wasted money grubstaking any miner who came to his general store for a loan, Augusta kept the household better than out of debt. As the years of high-altitude striving and hardship passed, she realized that her overgenerous husband was not apt to strike it rich. She did not complain. She gave him all she had to give because she knew that he was a good man.

While Tabor waited for his bonanza in Oro City, John Evans toiled on in his admirable indoor way for his own advancement and that of his community. He founded Colorado Seminary of the Methodist Episcopal Church in 1864, but the financial stagnation forced it to close soon. (It would reopen in 1880 as the University of Denver.) He pushed hard for the admission of Colorado Territory to the Union, which would lead to fulfillment of that old yearning of his—a Senate seat. The effort embroiled him for years in a tangle of thrusts and counterthrusts by lobbyists in Washington and by partisans in Colorado. The statehood process required an enabling act by Congress and creation of a state constitution and the selection of a slate of state and congressional officers to be passed on by the Colorado electorate. In 1864 Congress granted Evans's request for an enabling act, being eager for two new Republican senators to insure enough electoral votes for Lincoln's re-election and to help push reconstruction legislation through the Senate. But Colorado's voters turned down statehood, fearing taxes and military conscription.

A year later the same electorate barely approved statehood, helped, the Democrats said, by the fraudulent Republican votes of inebriated Ute Indians corralled in the saloons of Denver's

Blake Street. The slate of officers included Evans and Jerome
B. Chaffee as U.S. senators. The nominee for governor was
William Gilpin, who hoped to talk himself back into office
while proving up a Spanish land grant in San Luis Valley.
Jerome Chaffee was a smooth, tough, grizzly bear of a man
who made people wince when he shook their hands. He had
wrung a small fortune out of gold milling (crushing the gold ore
with iron stamps and removing it from the crushed rock by
amalgamation with mercury) in Gregory Gulch. Thereafter he
rose rapidly to power in the Evans orbit as a founder of the First
National Bank of Denver.

So the voters of the territory approved statehood—but Lin-
coln was in his grave by then. President Andrew Johnson, a
Democrat, was threatened by impeachment, and he had no use
for any more Republican senators to vote him out of office.
Through Johnson's opposition, Congress denied statehood to
Colorado that year and again in 1866. Meanwhile, Evans and
Chaffee considered themselves to be duly elected U.S. senators.
They were addressed as such by friends, maintained quarters in
Washington, wore somber black frockcoats, and appeared occasionally in the Senate chamber, where they were ignored by
the regular members. The dogged Evans made one last statehood effort in 1868. He failed again—not through the skulduggery of Andrew Johnson but through the treachery of another influential Colorado Republican, Henry Moore Teller, a
thirty-eight-year-old lawyer from Central City. Teller told
Congress that Colorado was disqualified from statehood because
it had less than half the 75,000 population that Evans and Chaffee claimed for it. Teller's real objection to statehood—with
Evans and Chaffee as U.S. senators—was something else. He
wanted to be a senator himself.

Henry Teller was born of Dutch ancestry on a farm in western
New York. He was quiet, studious, and reserved—a teetotaler
whose high moral principles were written in his pale, austere

face and shock of stiff brown hair rising from his high forehead. At the Republican convention of 1860 in Illinois he met Sam Elbert, who infected him with the Pikes Peak gold fever. He hurried to Central City and, having a gift of leadership, soon was in command of the Republicans of Gilpin County from Nevadaville down through Gregory Gulch to Black Hawk. As a lawyer he made money defending and contesting for his miners the singular Colorado law of apex, which ruled that if a gold-bearing vein surfaced on a man's claim, he could follow that vein all the way to China even though it passed out of the bounds of his claim into other claims.

Young Teller had a patron named William Austin Hamilton Loveland, a storekeeper who had helped to found the town of Golden. Everything about Loveland was mysterious and romantic. He was alleged to have been born in Massachusetts in 1826, to have stormed Chapultepec with General Scott in the Mexican War, to have lost a fortune or two as a California Forty-Niner, to have had a role in William Walker's seizure of Nicaragua in 1855 and in Cornelius Vanderbilt's unsuccessful scheme to put a canal across the Nicaraguan isthmus. He was tall, narrow-hipped, broad-shouldered and with a striking profile. There was about him something that suggested the sweep and beauty of the pass above Georgetown that bears his name. That name would be applied also to a mountain, a park, a fire station, and a town which has made a business of postmarking cards on Valentine's Day with its "Loveland" stamp.

Loveland's Golden stood at the point where Clear Creek tumbled out of the mountains. Its citizens fought bitterly with those of Denver for supremacy. (Denver and Golden shared the status of territorial capital until 1867 when Denver became the permanent capital.) Loveland directed the strategies of the so-called "Golden crowd" and did what he could to prevent "the Denver crowd," dominated by John Evans and Jerome Chaffee, from taking over the treasures of Gilpin County.

In 1861, Congress was planning a transcontinental railroad

from Omaha to San Francisco, to be built by two companies, Union Pacific and Central Pacific. Loveland was among those who urged the building of the Union Pacific part of this line through the Colorado Rockies—the old Frémont–Gilpin idea. The promoters hired the famous scout Jim Bridger and a young Swiss engineer Edward Louis Berthoud to find a feasible crossing of the Continental Divide from headwaters of Clear Creek above Golden to Middle Park, leading to Salt Lake City and California. Bridger and Berthoud did find a crossing—at 11,316 feet above sea level—and Berthoud wrote lyrical stories on the beauty of this Berthoud Pass for *The Rocky Mountain News*. But the railroad engineers wanted easy grades, not stuff for poetry—not wildflowers, avalanches, alpine tarns, exotic fauna, and uplifting vistas. In 1866 U.P. officials announced that the Union Pacific–Central Pacific would run from Omaha through the prairie settlement of Cheyenne, one hundred miles north of Denver.

The decision only increased Loveland's determination to put a railroad over Berthoud Pass. He acquired a territorial charter for what would be called the Colorado Central and Pacific Railroad, to run from the U.P. tracks at Cheyenne to Golden and then, by a mere spur, to Denver, signifying the demotion of that would-be metropolis to the status of a suburb of Golden. The main line would proceed west from Golden over Berthoud Pass, by tunnel if necessary.

While Loveland scrambled for funds to build the Colorado Central, Evans and Chaffee prepared to meet this challenge of "the Golden crowd." They sent a twenty-five-year-old assistant cashier in Chaffee's bank, David Moffat, to New York to inform financiers that whereas Loveland was operating on a shoestring, they had the money and the political influence to bring rails directly into Denver not only from Cheyenne but from Kansas City also. Kansas City was the start of a line being built westward by John Charles Frémont who, as head of the Kansas Pacific Railroad, was recovering from defeats as a presidential nominee and Civil War general.

With mining at a standstill, the mid-1860s were bad years to be promoting anything in Colorado Territory. No one dreamed that salvation was on the way, particularly since it involved William Gilpin, regarded generally as the region's most harum-scarum character, even though Congress had finally redeemed some of his Civil War scrip. When in 1844 Gilpin had ridden Old Flash over Cochetopa Pass on his way back from Oregon, he had fallen in love with that million-acre San Luis Valley empire known as the Sangre de Cristo Grant lying between the Rio Grande and the crest of the Sangre de Cristos. Now, twenty years later, he bought the property from its owners, the heirs of the late Charles Beaubien, for $41,000 on easy terms. To make his payments, he planned to sell bits of it to those English and Dutch financiers who were becoming fond of speculation in Colorado lands and mines.

Gilpin believed that the grant was full of gold. In June of 1864 he hired an expert to evaluate its mineral wealth—a professor of chemistry at Brown University, Nathaniel P. Hill, who was in Colorado examining mines for a group of investors from his native New England. Hill, aged thirty-two, was far more than a chemistry teacher. His interests were global, his curiosity insatiable. He was an intellectual possessed of an excellent business sense and a passion for health nostrums—cayenne pepper to purify his drinking water, senna preserved in prunes to aid digestion, Perry Davis painkiller for headaches.

From the first, Professor Hill liked Gilpin and found him endlessly entertaining as they toured Gilpin County and then rode from Denver south over Sangre de Cristo Pass to San Luis Valley. However, Hill deplored the ex-governor's "habit of living on whiskey in homeopathic doses." In a letter to his wife, Alice, in Rhode Island, Hill described Gilpin's beloved ponies Toby and Fanny:

> . . . the ugliest, homeliest, and meanest little rats I ever saw. They are so little that you can lift them out of a mud hole with ease. They are so baulky that about once an hour they stop till they get ready to go. In addition to this virtue, they kick at every opportunity. But the

Gov. thinks they are splendid. . . . Gov. G. knows almost
everything, but he is the most impractical man I ever knew. When
driving, he talks incessantly. Part of the time I think he is talking to
me, part of the time to Toby and Fanny. The rest is soliloquy.[1]

The professor was not impressed by the mineral potential of
Gilpin's Sangre de Cristo Grant. But he saw a great future for
Gilpin County if he could find a smelting process to reduce its
difficult ores into concentrates of gold, silver, and copper. In
1865 he went to Central City again and made a side trip to
Horace Tabor's Buckskin Joe, to California Gulch and the Twin
Lakes area of the Upper Arkansas. This time he loaded into
wagons several tons of ore from Jerome Chaffee's Bobtail Mine
in Gregory Gulch and accompanied the load across the plains to
the Missouri and on by steamer to New Orleans and to Swansea
in South Wales, one of the world's top smelting centers. The
crossing must have been rough. Hill wrote to Alice, "I have
taken such a dislike to the Atlantic (I don't know that it hurts
the ocean any) that if I get safely home I will remain on that
side." [2]

While the Bobtail ore was being tested in Swansea, Hill settled down at Morley's Hotel in London and dined with men who
were interested in Gilpin County mines—international bankers
like J. S. Morgan (father of J. Pierpont Morgan) and George
Peabody, and speculators like William Blackmore, whose
brother Richard had just finished writing a novel that would
become an English classic—*Lorna Doone*. Hill was a good
tourist. He made the rounds of London's historic places and
rose one morning at dawn to watch the Oxford–Cambridge boat
race on the Thames. The race had to be held so early because
that was when the tide was right.

Hill did not neglect London's seamy side, hiring as escorts

1. Nathaniel P. Hill, Hill to his wife, 23 June 1864. *The Colorado Magazine*
33:251–252 (October 1956).

2. Hill, to his wife, 16 March 1866. *The Colorado Magazine* 13:167 (September
1936).

two police detectives to be sure that he missed nothing. He wrote to Alice that with their help he examined

> places where the well-dressed aristocratic thieves meet and also the places where only the lowest and most wretched vagabonds gather together to drink and gamble & revel. . . . We visited one place which they called a soup house, where it is said the meat used is principally horse and cat. Our evening labor closed by calls at some of the most noted dance houses, where you can see twenty or thirty objects having the form of women and as many drunken sailors illustrating the very lowest stages of degradation.

Perhaps to reassure Alice, Hill closed his London travelogue with:

> Nobody's morals were ever corrupted by going to such places. Good night, my precious wife. As I retire, thoughts of you and the children exclude all others.[3]

At Swansea early in April 1866, Hill received promising reports on the high gold content of the Bobtail ore and smaller Gilpin County specimens. The reporter Richard B. Pearce, a Cornish metallurgist in his thirtieth year, had built smelters on the Swansea pattern all over the world. He told Hill that such a process would work on the gold and silver ores of Colorado and that large profits could be made by shipping the concentrate— the matte—to Swansea to remove the precious metals. Pearce could not accept Hill's invitation to come to Colorado just then, but he produced a crew of Cornish experts. The professor hired the crew to construct a plant on a piece of land in Black Hawk at the foot of Gregory Gulch, which he had acquired for his New England backers.

Hill's Boston and Colorado smelter began treating ore in December 1867. The plant was a success almost from the start. An immediate effect was to stop the stampede of Denver businessmen north to the coming rail metropolis of Cheyenne—a stampede spurred by the arrival at Cheyenne in November of the

---

3. Hill, to his wife, 30 March 1866. *The Colorado Magazine* 34:195 (July 1957).

first Union Pacific train from Omaha. By spring, investment capital in quantity was arriving in Denver and its satellite towns from the East and from Europe—Civil War profits that had been piling up for years. The gentle professor from Brown University took in stride the revival of mining that he had created, though it meant exchanging a peaceful life of lectures and correcting papers into that of a leading Colorado industrialist.

The Hill smelter did far more than stimulate the dormant gold production of Gilpin County and the infant silver industry around Georgetown. It set the stage for the spread of Colorado mining on a large scale three hundred miles southward along the Continental Divide through the San Juan Mountains to New Mexico. There was a by-product. The technique of hard-rock mining improved as hundreds of Cornishmen—whose forebears had followed the craft in the tin mines of England for generations—flocked to the Pikes Peak country at the urging of Richard Pearçe, who would join them in Gilpin County soon. These "Cousin Jacks" with their picturesque dress and language and colorful singing and dancing brought a much-needed touch of gaiety to the drab mining camps.

The rejuvenation of Colorado mining in 1868 came at just the right time for railroad development—the first big technological step in reducing the vastness of the territory to a manageable dimension by reducing travel time and transport costs a thousand percent, lifting land values, removing what remained of the Indian menace. For two decades, politicians in Washington had been so preoccupied with trying to push rails from Omaha to San Francisco that they had tended to ignore the land between. Now Coloradans saw their chance to convince Congress that their region was too important to be bypassed.

The prospect inspired Loveland and Evans to intensify the rivalry between Golden and Denver. It was an uneven contest. Evans was known nationally because of his successful career in Illinois. Loveland was virtually unknown outside of Colorado.

After two years of striving, he made no progress in pushing his Colorado Central north from Golden toward Cheyenne, though he did complete a twelve-mile spur to Denver in 1870.

Meanwhile Evans and the rest of "the Denver crowd" organized on paper the Denver Pacific Railroad, a hundred-mile line to connect Denver with the U.P. at Cheyenne. Evans's plan was to have this vital link built with someone else's capital, as he was averse to risking his own. He made progress when he put together in Washington a lobby of Methodists who induced Congress to give the Denver Pacific a generous grant of land. Then Evans contracted with the builders of the Union Pacific, Credit Mobilier, to lay Denver Pacific tracks south from Cheyenne in exchange for a controlling interest.

But the corrupt Credit Mobilier defaulted on its contract while the D.P. tracks were a long way from Denver. It was the kind of imbroglio that Evans loved to resolve, working long hours in his office half buried in legal briefs, contracts, and correspondence. During his talks with Credit Mobilier, he had kept in touch with directors of the Kansas Pacific Railroad, which had been wandering west for years from Kansas City without being able to decide whether to head for California by way of Raton Pass or to veer north to a junction with the U.P. in Nebraska. Early in 1869 at a railroad shantytown called Sheridan, near the Colorado border, construction of the Kansas Pacific was halted while the directors went in search of funds.

John Evans was impressed by the K.P. director who was in charge of construction. His name was General William Jackson Palmer, a small, tidy Philadelphian who had served with distinction as leader of the Fifteenth Pennsylvania Volunteer Cavalry through the Civil War. When Congress rescued the Kansas Pacific by increasing its land grant, the company instructed Palmer to build the railroad into Denver rather than to California or Nebraska. The assignment caused Evans to hire Palmer to finish building the Denver Pacific into Denver.

Palmer took on his double task in July 1869. He had some

fifty miles of gap to close in the Denver Pacific and one hundred and seventy-five miles of Kansas Pacific to build across the Colorado plains. By putting every idle teamster and laborer in the territory to work, Palmer brought trains from Cheyenne into Denver on June 17, 1870. He shifted these men at once to building east from Denver toward the west-building Kansas Pacific crews. A race ensued, during which it became commonplace for the rival crews to lay a mile of track in a single hour. On August 15, the entire Denver population gathered at the depot of the two railroad terminals to cheer the arrival of the first passenger train from Kansas City. Several of the cars were crammed with prostitutes, gamblers, and saloon men, who had been keeping the construction men entertained in railhead tent towns through the years as the K.P. rails had inched toward the Rockies.

Some Colorado pioneers—John Evans and Jerome Chaffee, for example—remained Easterners in their outlook—cautious, down-to-earth, unresponsive to the charm of their environment. William Jackson Palmer was not like them in spite of his fox-hunting dress and courtly Philadelphia manner. In 1867 the young general had made a four-thousand-mile horseback trip to Southern California and back past Pikes Peak, surveying for the Kansas Pacific. The trip had transformed him into as dedicated a mountaineer as Kit Carson and William Gilpin.

At the age of thirty-three, Palmer was a split personality. He had a poet's idealism combined with a hard-as-nails gift for corporate management. His poet's eye and his keen commercial sense made him see values in the grandeur of the high Rockies that few pioneers had perceived before him—the ingredients of a resort industry such as that which was emerging back East because of the affluence and leisure created by Civil War profits. Palmer believed that Colorado's setting was at least as attractive as the country around Newport, Rhode Island, or Saratoga, New York, or the various springs of Virginia. He was aware also that Colorado Territory was becoming known as a health center with a climate where consumptives and asthmatics found cures, where people survived horrible accidents such as Pegleg Smith the trapper had survived in North Park in 1828 by sawing off his own leg after it was shattered by an Indian's bullet.

Palmer's resort dream was heightened by a romantic involvement. In the spring of 1869 he became engaged to a nineteen-year-old debutante from Flushing, Long Island, named Queen Mellen, a girl he had met on the New York–St. Louis train. Queen was not the outdoor type. She hoped secretly that her dynamic fiancé would take a soft job as head of the Kansas Pacific office in New York so that she could begin a career as a patroness of the arts and a leader of Long Island society. But her husband-to-be had quite different ideas. When the directors of the Kansas Pacific turned down his recommendation that they build the road on over Raton Pass and on to California, he became a bitter critic of Eastern rail executives, whom he considered to be cynical, corrupt, and opposed to the public good. His distaste for a Long Island career was implied when he wrote to Queen: "I find myself doubting that a kind Providence ever intended man to dwell on the Atlantic slopes." [4]

He wrote his beloved almost daily of the delights he had found at the foot of Pikes Peak, of the soda springs and the eerie beauty of the Garden of the Gods, of the tailor-made resort that he intended to build near it, of their wilderness home "where the Monument or Fountain comes leaping from the cavernous wall of the Rocky Mountains." His letters contained paragraphs like these:

> Could one live in constant view of these grand mountains without being elevated by them into a lofty plane of thought and purpose? And then our future home occurred to me, and I felt so happy that I would have such a wife who was broad enough, earnest enough,

4. John S. Fisher, *A Builder of the West* (Caldwell, Idaho: The Caxton Printers, 1939), p. 150.

wise and good and pure enough to think that a wild home amidst such scenery was preferable to a brown stone palace in a fashionable city; to go out each evening on some neighboring hill and find each time a new vision of beauty and grandeur! [5]

In his missive of January 17, 1870, to Queen, he described the commercial part of his plans:

I had a dream last evening while sitting in the gloaming at the car window. I mean a wide-awake dream. Shall I tell it to you? I thought how fine it would be to have a little railroad a few hundred miles in length, all under one's own control with one's friends, to have no jealousies and contests and differing policies. . . . In this ideal railroad all my friends should be interested. . . . I would have every one of these, as well as every other employee on the Road, no matter how low his rank, interested in the stock and profits so that each and all should feel as if it were their own business. . . . Then I would have a nice house-car made, just convenient for you and me, with perhaps a telegraph operator and secretary, to travel up and down when business demanded. . . . [6]

Palmer began building his "little railroad" south from Denver on July 28, 1871, some months after marrying Queen. His conception was totally Western. Other railroad men of the period thought only of money to be made by transcontinental east-west traffic. Palmer's scheme was to connect the Colorado Rockies with lands to the south—to exploit the ancient Spanish trade routes between the South Platte and the Mexican border. He called his line the Denver and Rio Grande Railroad, projected from Denver to Pueblo, up the Arkansas beyond the Royal Gorge, over Poncha Pass to San Luis Valley and the Rio Grande, and down that stream to El Paso, Texas. Spur tracks from every Colorado mining district would descend the mountain streams to join the main line.

Half of Palmer's financial supporters were Philadelphians who had served under him through the Civil War. Others were

---

5. Fisher, *Builder of the West*, p. 178.
6. Fisher, *Builder of the West*, p. 177.

Englishmen with interests in Gilpin's Sangre de Cristo Grant and in the adjacent Maxwell Grant, which had been owned until 1870 by Lucien Maxwell. These Englishmen believed that Palmer's road would increase the value of their lands by passing near them. The tracks of the D. and R.G. arrived at Palmer's three-month-old dream town under Pikes Peak in October 1871. In another year trains were running to Pueblo to start the transformation of that sleepy adobe town of seven hundred people into the industrial metropolis of southern Colorado. The general had named his resort Colorado Springs even though it had no springs, because that was the fashionable thing to do. Many of its early residents were English, sent by investors in London to keep an eye on Palmer's projects, which was why the place acquired the nickname "Little London."

As an experiment in public transportation, the Denver and Rio Grande was a striking example of how the territory challenged its people to be innovative. Its gauge was narrow—rails three feet apart instead of the usual four-foot-eight-inch standard gauge. Its tiny locomotives and gold-painted cars were so light that a strong wind could blow them off the track. But lightness permitted grades as steep as six percent compared to the three percent maximum of standard-gauge lines. Curves could be so sharp that a locomotive could pass its own caboose—a feat that made for cheaper construction as the rails wound around narrow gulches.

Though the panic of 1873 stopped Palmer from getting his little trains along to Texas, he would push them into the most rugged parts of the Colorado Rockies at higher altitudes than rails had ever been pushed before, including crossing the Sangre de Cristos at La Veta Pass (9,383 feet above sea level) and the Continental Divide at Marshall Pass (10,846 feet). Their comic huffing and puffing had a great deal to do with the growth of the territory and the founding of towns, leading to statehood and a five-fold increase in Colorado's population and wealth.

4

And Statehood
—at Last

$\mathcal{T}$HE boom of the 1870s forced the development of radical new ways of producing food to meet the increased demands of the territory. There had been no such urgency through most of the doldrums of the first decade. As early as 1861 surprising amounts of everything from pork to celery were reaching the gold camps of Gilpin County and South Park from irrigated farms and grist mills in the San Luis Valley and on the Huerfano, Cucharas, and Purgatoire rivers just north of Raton Pass and the trading camp of Trinidad. Water-powered mills popped up all along the Front Range from Pueblo on the Arkansas to the army post and village of Fort Collins on the Cache la Poudre. Many miners gave up scratching for gold to become prosperous truck farmers around Denver and Boulder. Stockmen built the first herds of beef cattle by collecting oxen that had been abandoned by their owners after hauling the wagons across the plains from the Missouri. It had been supposed that these oxen would perish during the Colorado winters. But the same brown, air-cured grasses, buffalo and grama, that had been sustaining millions of buffalo sustained the oxen also. Native hay in the high valleys was harvested to feed dairy cattle. By 1867 alfalfa from

Mexican seed was being raised on Clear Creek, and steam machines were used to thresh homegrown wheat eastward along the South Platte to Fort Morgan and beyond.

John Evans and William Byers were the champions of Colorado farming in the 1860s. Byers, who had grown up on a farm in Ohio, filled *The Rocky Mountain News* with advice about raising crops in a mile-high land of scant rainfall and a short season. He argued that the South Platte and Arkansas valleys would grow anything that grew in the midwest, but that farming in Colorado was quite different, requiring co-operative study and irrigation. He stressed the prime fact of life in Colorado, the scarcity of water, and strongly supported the doctrine of prior appropriation, which had been legalized in 1866 by the territorial legislature and Congress. This "Colorado doctrine," adopted later throughout the Rockies, was based on the principle that the first person to file a claim to a farm along a stream had priority over later claimants to the beneficial use of that water during times of low flow when there was not enough water in the stream for everybody.

In 1863, Byers put together the Colorado Agricultural Society to promote methods adapted to the environment. Three years later he organized an agricultural fair where fifteen-pound turnips and fifty-bushel-an acre wheat were displayed. Neither the society nor the fair was a roaring success. The men who had rushed to Pikes Peak during the gold rush for adventure and freedom were suspicious of anything as socialistic as co-operation and were uninclined to give up practices that their fathers had taught them back in the humid East.

It took another journalist—and in the nick of time—to bring changes to keep pace with the expanding demand of the 1870s. His name was Nathan Cook Meeker, and he was an original like Frémont, Gilpin, and Palmer, but of a wilder cast than any of these. Many influences had shaped him. His career had ranged from farm boy to Greenwich Village poet, to reporter on the *New Orleans Picayune,* to traveling salesman, to novelist writing of supermen resembling himself who led barbarians out of savagery, to Civil War correspondent for Horace Greeley and his *New York Tribune*. Meanwhile, Meeker trained himself to become a professional idealist by studying the Utopian communes of the day—those of the Brook Farm transcendentalists, the Mormons, the Fourierites, and Campbellites, all of whom planned to eliminate vice and violence, suppress idlers, replace government by group effort, and combine the joy of sex with practical eugenics to improve the breed.

After the war, the tall and handsome Meeker came to New York as agricultural columnist for the *Tribune*. Horace Greeley shared Meeker's interest in Utopia and encouraged him to use the *Tribune* to promote an agrarian community of "temperance, monogamy, and religious tolerance" [1] where each member worked for the common good at the task he enjoyed doing most. Late in 1869, Greeley sent his idealist west by the Kansas Pacific, which ended near the eastern border of Colorado, to prepare articles about the territory and to look around for a farm tract on which to place what Socialist Meeker called Union Colony. William J. Palmer happened to be on the same K. P. train. He filled Meeker with his euphoria about Pikes Peak—the outpouring of a young man in love—as the two men rode in a spring wagon from the K. P. railhead near the Colorado–Kansas line across the rolling prairie to the general's site for Colorado Springs at the Front Range. Moving on from there past Castle Rock to Denver, Meeker ran into more euphoria, supplied this time by William Byers, who was marketing lands for John Evans fifty miles out on the flats east of Longs Peak near the junction of the South Platte and Cache la Poudre river—lands owned by the Denver Pacific Railroad. Byers lectured Meeker on the importance of irrigation and advised him to reject Palmer's valley at Pikes Peak as a location for Union Colony because

1. This phrase appeared in Meeker's famous "call," published in the *New York Tribune*, 14 December 1869.

it was too small and too short of water for large-scale farming, though he conceded that it would do for idlers who loved scenery and did not have to work for a living. Byers added that he had for sale a twelve-thousand-acre tract on the Cache la Poudre at five dollars an acre that would be just right for a colony.

Meeker was the most widely read farm columnist in the nation. When, on December 14, 1869, he issued in the *New York Tribune* his famous "call" for subscribers to join Union Colony at one hundred and fifty-five dollars a head, more than two hundred Easterners signed up. That was twice the number needed to buy the Denver Pacific tract. By spring many of them had arrived on the Cache prepared to turn the barren prairie into the Garden of Eden that Meeker had depicted in his "call." He named the place Greeley in honor of his patron. Each colonist received a town lot for his paid-up membership and one hundred and sixty acres of bottom land near town.

Most of the members were people of means and education, with skills representing every craft. Among them was a town planner General Robert A. Cameron, Brooklyn-born and bibulous, and a thoroughly trained water expert E. S. Nettleton, who had invented a device for measuring stream flow. Nettleton had studied the development of irrigation from its legendary beginnings under Adam and Eve through its use milleniums ago along the Nile and Euphrates and in India, China, Italy, and Spain. He had learned that similar methods, crude but workable, were used by the Pueblo Indians on the Rio Grande and by the Mexican-Americans of southern Colorado.

But he recognized in the rich, flat land around Greeley a new and exciting farming potential. The Cache la Poudre had its origin high in the Continental Divide only one hundred miles from Greeley—far too short a distance for that stream to collect enough irrigation water by rainfall in the way that the interminable Nile collected it. However, the combination of a remarkably porous granite soil, held in place by heavy forestation, and the tendency of rain and snow clouds blown east from the Pacific to dump their moisture when they struck the divide created a unique storage basin in the timberline area of the high country. The snow melted slowly in the cool temperatures of timberline and was held back also by the spongelike soil from which it filtered down to the plains around Greeley at a regular rate during most of the year. Nettleton believed that such irrigation, derived from the even flow of snow water through the growing season, would spare farmers of Union Colony many of the problems of erratic rainfall that plagued agriculture back East.

He observed further that truck farmers around Denver and Golden raised their crops only in the narrow bottomlands of streams, using irrigation from short ditches of a few hundred yards. The greater part of the snow water in those streams was not put to use. It flowed on to benefit the farmers of Kansas, and that, Nettleton felt, was a crime. He proposed to make fuller use of the Cache la Poudre as it flowed through Greeley by bringing some of its water to the semiarid benchlands, that is, to the level plain proper stretching back from and above the narrow bottomlands. He argued that Meeker's colonists could achieve this by building elaborate ditches—canals actually—running parallel to the river but falling at a more gradual rate than the ten-foot-per-mile fall of the river.

The principle was simple—the same that would be adopted thirty years later by the U. S. Bureau of Reclamation for all the mountain states. As Nettleton explained it to Meeker, the colony's irrigation ditches would start at points far up the Cache that were at higher altitudes above sea level than the altitude of the Greeley benchlands. As a result, the water diverted by the canals from the river would flow down to irrigate many thousands of acres of barren bench.

Nathan Meeker, like William Gilpin, had no love for manual labor. He preferred to talk about it—to instill in others the spirit of co-operation to get community projects done. His disciples responded well in the fall of 1870. Nettleton's Canal Number Two was thirty-six miles long and thirty-two inches wide on the bottom when they completed digging it two years later. Two more "high line" canals were dug by these charter members of Union Colony. Though the grasshopper plague of 1873 blurred the success of the Greeley experiment, the canal plan revolutionized high-altitude agriculture in time, raising Colorado farm production in a few years to an equal footing with mining and manufacture. Through the 1870s, similar long canals were built by other co-operative groups along the Front Range, including the Chicago-Colorado Colony, founders of Longmont (1870) on the Middle St. Vrain, and a group at Fort Collins (The fort there was abandoned in 1871.) on the Cache above Greeley. Soon it was hard to tell what was canal and what was river in that part of Weld County, a condition that prevails today.

Nettleton's advanced hydrology was practiced as far away as San Luis Valley, where colonies of Mormons set up the towns of Manassa and Sanford in the late 1870s. Developers from the East and from Europe began investing money in ditch companies to sell water to farmers far down the South Platte and the Arkansas—water that would bring about during the 1880s the creation of prosperous farm communities like Sterling and Rocky Ford. Some men foresaw that more water than the mountains of the eastern slope could provide would be needed to nourish all the prairie lands that incoming homesteaders hoped to reclaim. This sent them scurrying along the Continental Divide as nimbly as the gold seekers of 1859 in search of low places where Pacific slope water might be persuaded to flow to the Atlantic side in ditches or tunnels. A low point in the divide that held special promise was where the source of the Colorado approached, at Milner Pass, the source of the Cache and also of the Big Thompson, a branch of the Cache, in present Rocky Mountain National Park. This dream of transmountain water diversion in that vicinity would reach its fantastic fulfillment with the federal Colorado–Big Thompson project of the 1930s.

Not even Nettleton or William Byers visualized the wider significance of the Greeley irrigation program. It took the president of the United States to spell it out. In his annual message to Congress on January 1, 1873, Ulysses S. Grant said:

> Between the Missouri River and Rocky Mountains there is an arid belt of public land from 300 to 500 miles in width, perfectly valueless for occupancy of man for want of sufficient rain to secure the growth of any agricultural products. The irrigating canal would make productive a belt of country as wide as the supply of water could be made to spread over, and would secure a cordon of settlements connecting the present population of the mountain regions with that of the older states.[2]

President Grant could have put it another way. The canals on the Greeley pattern, reaching farther and farther eastward, marked the beginning of the end of the "great American desert," the answer to Major Long's insulting phrase, which had curbed interest in the plains of Colorado for half a century. It took many more years for people generally to believe that much of that wasteland could be brought to bloom. Birds from the woodland east were more perceptive. As early as the summer of 1886, a cardinal from Missouri was spotted looking over Fort Morgan on the South Platte, and a pair of mocking birds came to Rocky Ford to nest in a cottonwood on the Arkansas.

As the rugged individualists on farms along the rivers below the Front Range buckled down to co-operative irrigation, other entrepreneurs developed the exact opposite of co-operation to build a grasslands industry as feudal as the princedoms of the Middle Ages.

The princes of the open-range cattle business of the 1870s and 1880s worked by divine right, made their own laws, and asked permission of nobody to hold absolute sway over the public domain of the high plains from West Texas and New Mexico to Canada. This neo-feudalism, American style, came about by accident—a unique regional sideshow of the national

2. Fritz, *Colorado*, p. 330.

circus. Two ephemeral conditions created it. There on the plains were half a million square miles of short grass free for the eating. Most people thought of the area as a lonesome, worthless, arid vastness to be crossed and forgotten with all possible speed. Condition two was the presence, down in the West Texas brush, of an Anglo-Spanish blend of cattle called longhorns, descended from those the *conquistadores* had brought from Andalusia to the New World in the sixteenth century. The techniques of the Texas cowboys to manage the modern longhorns were as Spanish as the cattle. Even the language was Iberian—words like *bronco*—Spanish for "rough" or "crabbed"; *sombrero,* from "sombra" ("shade"); *remuda,* meaning "change" or "replacement."

They were bovine terrors, these longhorns—temperish, ugly, and with horns spreading five feet across. They were as erratic as heat lightning, and they carried disease with no noticeable ill effects. Their hides were so tough that snakes and insects and thorns and buckshot bothered them not at all. Before the Civil War, Texas stockmen had shipped them to cities up the Mississippi to be sold as beef—not tasty but at least edible. That market ended when Union forces won control of the river.

With nowhere to go, the longhorns multiplied, and the grass of Texas on which they fed began to give out. At war's end, a few drovers discovered that the starving animals gained weight on the prairie grasses even while they were being driven a thousand miles north to be sold at the railheads of the Kansas Pacific and other lines advancing into Colorado. They cost the drovers very little. Colorado stockmen paid well for them, planning to upgrade them with Eastern bulls and sell the progeny to hungry miners, to railroad construction crews, and to army garrisons guarding the Union Pacific in present Wyoming.

John Wesley Iliff, who would rule briefly as king of the Colorado plains, was twenty-eight years old when he reached Denver in 1859 with wagonloads of food to sell to the swarm of gold seekers. He had no beef at first but got some soon from those discarded oxen of the Argonauts. Iliff arranged to look like General Grant, as many admirers of the little hero tried to do, and he possessed the trademark of the Colorado pioneer— the ability to invent ways to make money out of the disadvantages of the environment.

He was Scotch, monosyllabic, shrewd, pious enough to live up to the name of the founder of Methodism, and so reserved as to be the least known of Colorado's innovators. He had no revealing idiosyncrasies, though he had a passion for eating chestnuts, and he smoked cigars incessantly. He did commit one surprisingly unreserved act. While riding in his buggy from his ranch to Denver, he picked up a hitchhiker from Pueblo named Lizzie Frazier, who was handling a line of Singer sewing machines. Against his Scotch instincts he bought a Singer, which he didn't need, from this fascinating salesperson and consummated the purchase later by marrying Lizzie.

As his breeding herd increased, Iliff grazed the cattle farther and farther east on the unfenced, free grass of the South Platte River valley from which, providentially for him, the hostile Cheyennes and the buffalo were withdrawing. But he could not raise beef fast enough to meet the terms of his beef contracts. In 1866, longhorn cattle began to be heard and seen bawling and brawling around Denver. Iliff bought some cows from a drover named Goodnight, and found that the quality of their calves improved when he bred them to his shorthorn bulls imported from Illinois.

Charles Goodnight, an enormous, Kentucky-born centaur of a stockman, had been in Texas since 1845 and had fought Indians and Union soldiers as a Confederate Texas Ranger. He was renowned for honesty and he knew as much about handling wild longhorns and wild cowboys on those cattle drives north on the Chisholm Trail to Abilene, Kansas, as any man alive. In 1866 Goodnight and Oliver Loving, who was briefly his partner, had decided to veer west into New Mexico to avoid the Comanche and Kiowa Indians who were harassing the cattle drives on the

Chisholm Trail. From the Staked Plains of Texas, they put some two thousand longhorns into Colorado by way of the Pecos River and Raton Pass instead of driving them up the Arkansas from Abilene.

The tough old mountain man Dick Wootton, who had a dubious claim to Raton Pass, charged toll to cross it, with six-gun in hand as proof of the legality of his claim. Next year, Goodnight avoided Wootton's toll by blazing what came to be called the Loving-Goodnight Trail past the beautiful volcanic cone Mount Capulin and over Trinchera Pass, some thirty-five miles east of Trinidad and Raton Pass (Ste. Rte. 389 today). He hoped that John Wesley Iliff would buy this big herd of longhorns, which he wintered on a ranch below the Spanish Peaks on Apishapa River. The cattle had cost Goodnight little more than the dollar-a-day wage for the dozen cowboys and the chuck-wagon cook that he had hired for the two-month drive from Texas. Iliff did want the two thousand cattle and paid Goodnight $20,000 for them, delivered at the Union Pacific corral in Wyoming.

That year, 1868, when the Hill smelter at Blackhawk was putting the gold camps of Colorado Territory on their primrose path to growth and prosperity, Iliff began expanding his lordly cattle kingdom right next door to Meeker's plebian Union Colony of farmers at Greeley. From near Denver, Iliff's domain would extend two hundred miles down the left, the north, bank of the South Platte almost to Julesburg and northward ninety miles across the dry, treeless prairie to the Union Pacific tracks in present southern Wyoming—most of Weld County as it was bounded then. His practice was to buy some twelve thousand longhorns annually from Goodnight or any other drover who could deliver them to what came to total 650,000 acres of U. S. property in Colorado under his rule. The average weight of each ten-dollar steer was six hundred pounds. After feeding for two years on the government's grass, the steer weighed a thousand pounds and sold for thirty-five dollars—a total profit to Iliff for the year's sales, after negligible expenses, of as much as one

hundred twenty thousand dollars—enough to make him a mil-
lionaire before he died in his prime, aged forty-six years, in
1878. Long after his death, in 1903, his widow Lizzie and his
children founded and endowed the Iliff School of Theology,
which thrives in Denver still.

Through the 1870s, Iliff bred his best longhorn cows to Eastern bulls until his upgraded breeding herd numbered twenty-five
thousand head. He maintained military control over his empire
by setting up nine ranches as headquarters for his armed fore-
men. His main headquarters were at the present town of Iliff.
The ranches amounted to fifteen thousand acres—sites selected
because they locked in the northside streams emptying into the
South Platte. The stretches of grassland between streams were
of no value unless the cattle grazing on them had access to the
water of the streams, an access which Iliff's cowboy knights
were careful to discourage by force. To acquire the strategic
ranches, Iliff paid his employees to pre-empt the land in 160-
acre parcels or to homestead it as stipulated in the Homestead
Act of 1862. When the employees received patents for the parcels after five years of alleged residency, they signed them over
to Iliff. This was not the way the Homestead Act was supposed
to work. But, it was almost routine in the nineteenth-century
West—the illegal means by which most of the public domain
of Colorado Territory found its way into private ownership.

The success of Iliff's South Platte empire inspired a flock of
imitators. Another shrewd Methodist John Wesley Prowers
began freighting as a teenager in 1856 for William Bent at his
second fort on the Arkansas. Prowers married a Cheyenne Indian girl, raised a family, and started a herd based on Herefords
shipped to him on the Santa Fe Railroad, which was headed for
California in the 1870s by way of the Arkansas and Raton Pass.
Within five years Prowers was grazing ten thousand cattle on a
forty-mile stretch of the public domain along the Arkansas east
of the present railroad division town of La Junta. Meanwhile,
the thought of being a cattle king enchanted many Europeans.

The same sort of Scots and English who had invested in General Palmer's railroad and in the Mexican land grants of Governor Armijo began setting up open-range empires which came in time to occupy most of the high plains. By 1875, foreign investors in Colorado alone had half a million beef cattle fattening on federal land. One of these empires, the Prairie Land Company established by Scotsmen, owned 150,000 head grazing on five million acres that did not belong to it in southern Colorado, New Mexico, and the Oklahoma Panhandle.

It was a strange development—this cattle autocracy. It could not last, though nobody foresaw the rapidity of its demise in less than two decades. To protect it a powerful lobby was formed in Denver inspired by the Colorado Stock Growers Association, which began in 1867. The association was not at all a co-operative in the sense of Meeker's Union Colony, but more of a baronial league on the order of those in fifteenth-century England during the Wars of the Roses. It accomplished little. Equally futile was the support of the president of the United States Rutherford B. Hayes, who had no success in 1877 when he asked Congress to reserve all the high plains west of the 100th meridian exclusively for stockmen.

Lobbies and presidents could not stop the course of adverse events. The price of longhorns rose as the oversupply in the Texas brush disappeared. The prejudice against longhorns as bearers of disease resulted eventually in their legal banishment from Colorado. Higher grades of stock imported from the British Isles to improve profits—Galloways, Devons, Ayrshires—did not do well in the high altitude and rough winters of the Colorado plains. And it became clear that sheep were as fond of free public-domain grass as cattle. Though the wars between sheep men and cattlemen did not break out fully until 1880, the contention for use of the open range began years earlier. Cattlemen developed a pathological hatred of sheep people; they claimed that sheep killed the grass by cropping it too closely—a self-serving argument that was true only if their cattle had overgrazed the range in the first place. The conflict had racist over-tones because the first sheep attempting to invade the cattle kingdoms on the South Platte were brought in by Captain J. S. Maynard for his ranch north of Greeley. Though Maynard had bought his sheep back East, some cattlemen assumed that they came from those native Mexican-Americans of Southern Colorado who had been raising them in San Luis Valley and north of Raton Pass since the 1840s. That is one reason why today's Mexican-Americans in the counties south of the Arkansas still vote solidly Democratic, as they did a century ago in reaction to the Republicanism of the Anglo stockmen in the Front Range cities to the north.

The crowning blow to the open-range industry was fore-shadowed not by Coloradans but by that voluble, if absentee, member of Union Colony Horace Greeley, who sent a carload of fruit trees to Greeley from Virginia which, he hoped, would give his prairie town out West the soft and fragrant look of the Old South. When the cattle of the colonists devoured the young trees, Greeley advanced twenty-five thousand dollars to buy fifty miles of smooth-wire fence to hold the cattle in their com-mon pasture.

The smooth wire was a failure, but a few years later, in 1874, Joseph Glidden, an Illinois farmer, got a federal patent on a new kind of fence wire carrying sharp barbs, which he had invented to keep his dogs out of Mrs. Glidden's flower beds. When Texans found that the barbs would hold even their intractable longhorns, its use spread over the high plains. Homesteading farmers enclosed their tracts with it to keep the open-range cattle from invading their fields. But the cattle kings had to have a fenceless terrain for successful trail drives. They began cutting the fences and ordering the "nesters" away at gunpoint, declar-ing that the range belonged to them. Their claims did not hold up in court, and the farmers with their fences and irrigation ditches were numerous enough soon to match force with force. The free range was reduced further when the railroads began fencing their rights of way—a policy adopted because the open-range stockmen lobbied through a law making the railroads liable for cattle struck by their trains. The fencing was cheaper than paying damages for the stricken cattle, which always turned out to be the most valuable that the complaining owner possessed.

The sick industry stumbled along through the early 1880s, during which the larger cattle companies learned how to balance their books by enlarging their inventory—counting each of their cattle twice or thrice. That dodge could not be used after the tragic winter of 1886–1887 when half of all the open-range stock perished in blizzards and deep snow throughout the plains. Only a few outfits survived to continue business on fenced ranches, raising hay to feed a better grade of cattle in winter and providing shelters for their survival.

Some open range remained after 1887, but the magic chain was broken—the chain of longhorns, limitless grass, advancing railroads, a surplus of investment capital, fewer hostile Indians. Only the legends survived—tales of cowboys and their wonderful world of space and self-reliance, brave cowboys surviving stampedes and floods, carefree cowboys at the spring and fall roundups, reverent cowboys stammering with shyness in the presence of pure women, imperturbable cowboys chasing rustlers with six-guns smoking, handsome cowboys living it up in the dance halls and gambling dens of the railroad towns.

The mining revival, the coming of railroads, expanded irrigation, the open-range industry, the population surge—all these things made statehood inevitable during the 1870s, though there were zigs and zags to confuse the issue. Opponents of the territorial system called it "carpet-bag government"—meaning rule by those they called "wind-broken blatherskites" sent west by President Grant to pay off political debts. Some of the anti-statehood people feared that higher taxes would result. Some of them were unreconstructed Southern Democrats who objected to the congressional requirement that the new Colorado state con-

stitution must give Negroes the right to vote, which had not
been stipulated in the earlier constitutions. But the new state
would gain enormous riches. Two sections (six hundred and
forty acres each) of the federal domain in each of the thousands
of Colorado townships could be sold to pay for public schools,
fifty sections of land would provide for administrative buildings,
and fifty sections for a state penitentiary. Seventy-two sections
more would be given on which to build the University of Colorado at Boulder—the institution which had existed only on
paper since its creation by the territorial legislature in 1861.

Jerome Chaffee, a polished multimillionaire now, who
bought his clothes and had his beard trimmed in New York, was
still promoting statehood and dreaming of really being the U. S.
senator that he had pretended to be in the 1860s. He had become an astute wheelhorse politician both in Denver and in
Washington as territorial delegate to Congress. He controlled all
the Colorado Republicans except the Gilpin County crowd at
Central City who followed Henry Teller, a man to be feared
because of his unblemished character and skill as an orator.
Chaffee enjoyed prestige as one of President Grant's com-
panions at White House poker games where national policy was
said to be decided between deals. All the while, John Evans
gave Chaffee powerful support, though discreetly, realizing at
last that the taint of the Sand Creek affair had ruined his own
ambitions to be a senator. In 1873 Chaffee persuaded Grant to
name Evans's faithful son-in-law Sam Elbert as territorial governor, replacing Grant's corrupt comrade-at-arms at Shiloh,
General Edward McCook. Ten months later, or so the story
goes, Chaffee angered the president by filling an inside straight
over Grant's three-of-a-kind. The pot was large, and the alleged
outcome was that poor Elbert, an honest, well-meaning man,
found himself out of office and McCook back in just as Sam
was beginning to enjoy the governorship.

Coloradans regarded the reinstatement of McCook as carpet-
baggery at its worst. They had had quite enough of the plausible

McCook during his first governorship, disliking his elegance, his waxed handlebar moustache, even his beautiful bride, Mary Thompson, whom he imported from Peoria, Illinois. Mary was criticized because she wore low-necked gowns and too many jewels at parties. Gossips declared—out of jealousy, no doubt— that she fainted prettily at Denver's American House ball in 1872 honoring Grand Duke Alexis, brother of the Czar of Russia, only so that the glamorous Romanoff would come to her rescue by taking her in his arms.

McCook's brand of corruption was galling because it was hard to expose. His first act as governor in 1868 was merely an exercise of the usual nepotism. He put Mary's brother James Thompson, a playboy type, in charge of the Colorado Utes and made him his private secretary. Thompson delivered to the Utes as their annuity allotment a herd of scrawny longhorns which McCook bought at low prices. People said, but could not prove, that the governor billed the Indian Office in Washington for the longhorns at current high prices for "good Eastern cattle," which was the kind that the Utes were supposed to receive. Later, Mary's widowed sister Margaret came to Denver. To escape the expense of supporting Margaret, McCook found a husband for her—a big, muscular German who had changed his name from Carl Schwanbeck to Charles Adams. The governor got Adams the necessary salary by making him a general of militia, Indian agent for the White River Utes, and bodyguard to protect him from irate Utes who called at his office occasionally to complain about the scrawny longhorns.

The widespread protest over Sam Elbert's removal and Mc-Cook's reinstatement could not have pleased Jerome Chaffee more. It strengthened his statehood cause and brought a split between his Denver Republicans and those Republicans of Gilpin County under Teller, who was supporting McCook as a favor to President Grant. The split allowed the Democrats to elect in 1874 their first territorial delegate to Congress, a newcomer from Ireland named Thomas M. Patterson. That looked like a

Republican defeat, but it was really another Chaffee victory. It frightened the Republicans in Washington into passing an enabling act for Colorado statehood on March 3, 1875, on Chaffee's assurance that the new state's three electoral votes would go to the Republican candidate for president, Rutherford B. Hayes, who might need them to win. President Grant had already partially healed the Republican split in Colorado by removing McCook a second time as governor and sending in his place, pending statehood, a tactful and forthright Kentuckian by way of Illinois John L. Routt. Chaffee completed party unity by agreeing that Henry Teller would be one of the new U. S. senators and himself the other.

It was pure accident that Colorado came into the Union while the nation was celebrating its one-hundredth year, a coincidence which prompted general use of the nickname "the Centennial State." The proposed constitution gave male Negroes the right to vote, but the constitutional convention denied suffrage (24 to 8) to women of any color. The denial occurred even though the newly formed Colorado Women's Suffrage Association bombarded the convention with petitions from all sections of the territory "signed by ten thousand citizens." [3] Colorado women had come a long way toward independence since Julia Holmes's trek up Pikes Peak, and they urged the men to give Colorado the honor of being the first state in the Union to do what had to be done in all fairness. They pointed out that women in Wyoming Territory had had full voting rights since 1869 and would continue voting when that territory became a state. (In 1890 Wyoming did become the first state with full woman suffrage.) But Colorado's women lost their battle this time, partly because the convention was loaded with miners who believed that the hills were still man's preserve, and partly for fear that such an innovation would wreck the drive for statehood.

3. "Sorrows of the Suffragettes—1876," *Mountain and Plain History Notes* 13:1 (January 1976).

The males-only constitution was ratified by the people on July 1, 1876—15,443 for and 4,062 against. President Grant declared Colorado to be the thirty-eighth state on August 1. The national Republicans got their three electoral votes in the fall— votes which did give Hayes the presidency by a one-vote margin over the Democrat Samuel J. Tilden. Chaffee and Teller were admitted to the U. S. Senate, and Thomas Patterson to the House. John L. Routt won the governorship.

Routt designated July 4 as Colorado's festival day—"joy unrestrained" as *The Rocky Mountain News* put it, with bonfires and bands and exuberant drunks and meetings with long florid speeches. Down in Pueblo on the Arkansas, Charles Goodnight, a temporary resident, listened impassively to the oratory. With him were the men who financed his cattle drives, two young brothers from Pennsylvania, John A. and Mahlon D. Thatcher, who had begun selling ribbons and bows in the 1860s and then started the First National Bank of Pueblo because they owned the only safe on the Arkansas. At Colorado Springs, General Palmer watched the evening's fireworks on Pikes Peak from the Garden of the Gods. (His silken wife, Queen, had retired to Long Island, having failed to find the poetry in pioneering that Palmer had found.) Oro City below Mosquito Pass was in decline and had little to celebrate. Horace Tabor was fortyish now, and his face had the sag of a man who knew that wealth and romance had passed him by. He closed his store and spent the day keeping out of Augusta's way and speculating on where all the silver might be that people said was the coming thing.

Denver was the gay spot, with thousands lining the streets for the grand parade, including a band of Ute Indians, the men in stovepipe hats and frock coats, the women gowned in flour sacks. From the American House, the parade moved slowly to the picnic grove across the South Platte. Everybody had a band—the Pioneers, the Scandinavians, the German turners, the Masons, the Governor's Guards. The members of Colorado Commandery No. One were splendid on jet-black horses. The

Odd Fellows (purple uniforms) rode milk-white horses. The firemen, in patriotic red-white-and-blue uniforms, marched smartly. One great canopied float carried thirteen beautiful girls with flowers in their hair, representing the original thirteen states of 1776. Behind them came a float of thirty-eight girls— the thirty-eight states of 1876. They were posed gracefully around a fifteen-year-old Queen of Colorado, May Butler. May wore a robe of bunting with a high crown of gold on her head. She carried a golden wand.

It was all very thrilling, this statehood, and yet unsettling to some. How could all these things have happened in seventeen years—barely enough time to raise a child? Here was a vast and unknown wilderness transformed into a civilized land known the world over for its wealth and promise. Here was this site of Denver, once a barren plain for jackrabbits and yucca, magically become a city of 35,000 people bolstered by fast-growing satellites from Fort Collins and Longmont in the north to Pueblo, Walsenburg, and Trinidad in the south. Good and bad things had occurred—John Gregory's gold strike, the devastating Denver fire of 1863, the Cherry Creek flood a year later, the Sand Creek tragedy on the eastern plains, the financial crisis before Hill built his Gilpin County smelter, the success of the railroads and of Nathan Meeker's irrigation ditches.

Some of the leaders watching the July 4 parade had had their own good and bad times. John Evans had wanted to be a senator, but the voters had ruled against him. William Loveland had dreamed of winning fame and fortune as a railroad magnate until he and his Colorado Central became embroiled in the machinations of Jay Gould to control all the railroads in sight. The model husband William Byers found his career as Colorado's leading promoter threatened when a seductive milliner named Hattie Sancomb announced publicly (in revenge for his cooling ardor) that the two of them had been having an affair for years. And William Gilpin over there—as trim and oracular as ever, but betraying the frayed nerves of a henpecked husband.

The ex-governor had been a tranquil bachelor for fifty-nine years until 1874 when he succumbed to the charms of a widow from St. Louis, Julia Pratte Dickerson, who turned out to have a gift for creating domestic uproar.

After the statehood parade a depressing question occurred to some Coloradans as they strolled home. Where do we go from here? Was it a question of too much too soon?

5

"The Utes Must Go . . ."

SEVERAL months after Queen May Butler waved the golden wand over her happy subjects, many Coloradans began to think of their empire in terms of science and geography rather than as just so much rock that might be hiding gold and silver. The reason was the appearance, in 1877, of a mammoth publication twenty-seven inches from top to bottom and twenty inches wide, titled *Atlas of Colorado* with lithographs by Julius Bien. The publisher was the U. S. Department of the Interior. The author was Ferdinand Vandeveer Hayden, described in the frontispiece as "Geologist in Charge of the U. S. Geological and Geographical Surveys of the Territories."

Hayden was by no means the first to explore the Rockies with science in mind. Edwin James had scratched the surface during the Long expedition of 1820. Frémont's cartographer, Charles Preuss, had scratched a bit more, and so had Richard Kern, the astronomer with Captain Gunnison on the ill-fated Cochetopa Pass crossing of 1853. Of greater importance were the limited surveys along the fortieth parallel by Clarence King (1867–1872) and those by Lieutenant George M. Wheeler (1871–1877) in the San Juan country, both under auspices of the War Department. Meanwhile there were the expeditions of a brilliant ex-soldier Major John Wesley Powell, who had lost an

arm while fighting with Grant at Shiloh but did not let that
handicap him. In 1867 Powell climbed Pikes Peak and also Lincoln Peak in the Mosquito Range. His wife, Emma Dean,
climbed with him, proving once again what Julia Holmes had
proved on top of Pikes Peak in 1858.

Major Powell, William Byers, and their party in 1868 were
the first to climb Longs Peak. Powell spent that winter making
an ethnological study of the White River Utes on the western
slope. In the spring he began one of the great feats of American
exploration, the 900-mile descent by boat of the fearful gorges
of the Green and Colorado rivers, including Grand Canyon.
During the same summer Professor J. D. Whitney of Harvard
brought a group of his mining-school students to climb, measure, and name a cluster of peaks in the Sawatch Range, which
he called the Collegiates. The students were loyal fellows. They
named the highest of the Collegiates Mount Harvard, and con-
descended to call a lower peak Mount Yale. Later surveys
would show that Mount Harvard (14,420 feet) is third highest in
all the Rockies after Mount Elbert (14,433 feet) and Mount
Massive (14,421 feet) just north of it, up the Arkansas.

Major Powell pioneered the U. S. Geological Survey, but
Hayden's *Atlas of Colorado* was in a pioneer class by itself.
There had been earlier maps of the Rockies, of course, from the
crude drawings of the Dominguez–Escalante cartographer in
1776 to the maps of Colorado Territory made in 1861–1862 by
Governor Gilpin's surveyor general Francis M. Case, so that
Gilpin could lay out his first counties and Front Range townships. But none of the early maps of the West—or even of the
East—compared with the beautiful plates of the Hayden Atlas.
There were twenty sheets, mostly on a grand scale of four miles
to the inch. The maps had been drawn from triangulations made
by Hayden's engineers using fifty-pound theodolites—combined
transits and levels—which they lugged on foot to the dizzying
summits of the principal fourteen-thousand-foot peaks. The
triangulations were keyed to the forty-second parallel and to a

guide meridian at 104 degrees 30 minutes, which paralleled the Front Range just east of Denver and Colorado Springs.

An economic map in the atlas located the state's forests, pastures and croplands, its areas of coal, gold, and silver, its railroads inching their way into the hills toward the mining camps, and its network of toll roads. Among the roads shown was one running three hundred miles from civilization at Pueblo across Sangre de Cristo Pass and San Luis Valley and up the Rio Grande to a new silver camp in the San Juan Mountains called Silverton. The road crossed the Continental Divide at Stony Pass (12,594) which was only a little lower than the Mosquito Pass road connecting Fairplay and Horace Tabor's Oro City. A drainage map displayed accurately for the first time how the Colorado Rockies gathered waters that formed most of the major rivers of the West. Six geological maps in gorgeous reds, greens, blues, and yellows outlined the regions where ancient seas had laid down the sediments of future sandstones, and where volcanoes had erupted.

Dr. Hayden produced his maps with such accuracy, clarity, and knowledge that they survive in Colorado today as the ultimate authority. Modern measuring devices have brought little change to the altitude figures, which were determined a century ago using Hayden's instruments. The atlas, for example, put the height of Pikes Peak at 14,147 feet above sea level, Longs Peak at 14,271 feet, as compared with present official figures for Pikes Peak of 14,110 and for Longs Peak, 14,255—inconsequential variations.

One achievement of the atlas was to bring permanence to the existing nomenclature that had accumulated through the ages— Indian names like Uncompahgre (hot springs) River; Spanish names like Cucharas (spoon) River; many names for peaks and creeks with which the trappers of the 1830s had honored friends and animals; the later names concocted by the prospectors—Tarryall Creek, Hoosier Pass, Parrott City, Baker's Park. The atlas resolved confusion by establishing a single name for a

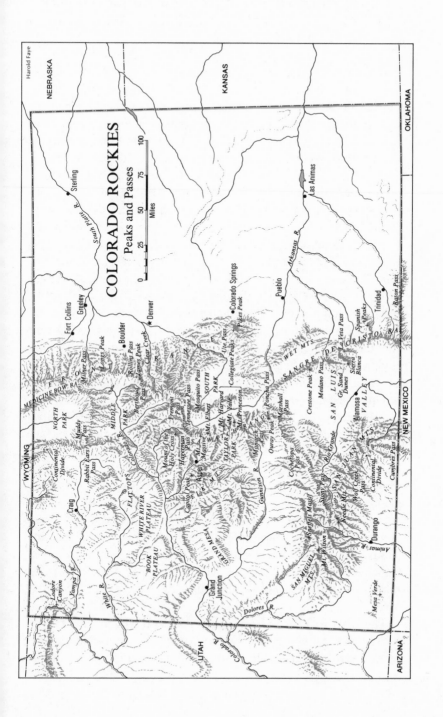

feature that had had several historically. It applied "Gunnison River" to the stream bordering the Elk Range on the south, which had been called Flintstone River or Eagle or Compadre. "Eagle River" was shifted to where it is now under Tennessee Pass. The ancient name "Bunkara" gave way to Roaring Fork.

Very few place names in the atlas have been discarded (Hayden's "Buckskin Peak" in the Mosquito Range is Mount Democrat now; "Union Park" is Taylor Park). Having put Governor Sam Elbert's name on the territory's highest peak, Hayden felt obliged to compliment Elbert's father-in-law, too, so we have that sedate pile southwest of Denver, Mount Evans. Countless landmarks had no names, but Hayden's young topographers applied them with gusto—"Mount Teocalli" in the Elks above "Coffee Pot Pass" where they had left a pot behind. They spattered their own names about generously—"Mount Wilson" in the San Miguels for Ada D. Wilson; "Marvine's Creek" for Archibald Marvine, who had been also with Professor Whitney's Harvard students in 1869. Marvine was a Princeton, not a Harvard, man, and he saw to it that the Hayden atlas had a Mount Princeton in the Collegiates along with Mount Harvard and Mount Yale. Since the men spent much time whirling socially in Colorado Springs, they showed their gratitude by naming a pinnacle south of Pikes Peak "Mount Rosa" after Rose Kingsley, the pioneering daughter of Charles Kingsley, canon of Westminster Abbey. Rose had come to Pikes Peak from England seeking adventure and to serve as a sort of director of social activities for General Palmer's resort. Her hobby was mountain climbing. The name "Cameron's Cone," near Mount Rosa was chosen to honor the Union Colony charter member General Robert A. Cameron, who had platted both Colorado Springs and Fort Collins after platting Greeley for Nathan Meeker.

Though the *Atlas of Colorado* was spectacular, its prime mover was as nondescript as someone's gone-to-seed uncle. F. V. Hayden, a small, mild-seeming creature addicted to frayed frock coats, battered hats, and fits of belligerence, grew up an orphan in Ohio, got a doctor's degree, but never found time to practice medicine. He began exploring the West in 1853 and had become a legend of physical stamina and scientific precision by 1872, when he surveyed and promoted in Congress the future Yellowstone Park, with his expenses paid by the same William Blackmore who had entertained Nathaniel P. Hill in London. After much work in the Yellowstone region, Hayden spent the summers of 1873, 1874, and 1875 directing four small parties of highly trained young men in the prodigious labor of mapping the Colorado Rockies.

Hayden differed from his colleague in western surveys John Wesley Powell. Whereas Powell stressed caution and realism in dealing with the arid environment, Hayden preferred to ignore the limitations. He resembled the nothing-is-impossible Gilpin in contending that Coloradans would find ways to overcome every obstacle so that they could enjoy the blessings of their earthly paradise. His quixotic optimism infected his youthful companions in exploration. Their exuberance and their love for the Rockies rubbed off, in turn, on the citizenry as their adventures were reported annually by the Department of the Interior. They gloried in their health and strength and in the trappings of romance—tattered clothes, ferocious beards, shoulder-length hair in the manner of the mountain men of old. They were too utterly absorbed in the wonders of each day—wonders of paleontology, botany, anthropology, ornithology—to notice dangers lurking about, such as hostile Ute Indians, electrical storms above timberline, rivers in flood, grizzly bears.

During their three summers in the field, Hayden's mountaineers visited every nook and cranny of the Colorado high country, from North Park and the Flat Tops surrounding Trappers Lake on south through the most rugged region of all, the San Juan Uplift, with its magnificent subranges, the Grenadiers, Needles, San Miguels, and the Sneffels Massif. They explored the precipitous Crestones in the Sangre de Cristos and were the first men of record to climb that towering guardian of San Luis Valley, Mount Blanca (14,363 feet). They virtually discovered major summits of the Elk Mountains, bestowing names on them designed to please Congressmen in Washington—Capitol Peak, Treasury Mountain, Whitehouse Mountain.

In 1874, the San Juan division of the survey, led by A. D. Wilson, stopped at the brand-new gold-silver camp of Lake City on the Lake Fork of Gunnison River. While there, one of the engineers proposed the name "Cannibal Plateau"—still in use—for the nearby ridge where Alfred Packer won immortality by allegedly eating the most appetizing parts of five friends who had become stranded with him on the ridge during the bitter winter of 1873–1874. Packer claimed in court later that his program was a practical exercise in survival. On this San Juan trip, the division's reporter and philosopher, Franklin Rhoda, struggled to the top of Mount Nebo and delivered a talk to the ptarmigans and pipits on the rapture one felt treading where no man had trod before, only to step, a moment later, on a whiskey bottle discarded earlier by a roving prospector.[1]

F. V. Hayden was the driving force behind these surveys, but another kind of genius, the photographer William H. Jackson, was the man who brought the work to worldwide attention. His photos of Two-Story House in present Mesa Verda National Park gave people their first views of the Pueblo Indians' civilization, which had flourished in cliff dwellings a thousand years ago. Jackson persuaded Chief Ouray and his superstitious Ute Indians to permit what they called his "evil eye" to record on wet plates their home life at Los Pinos Agency near Cochetopa Pass. Millions of readers thrilled to newspaper stories of how Jackson and his beloved mule Hypo survived a freezing night on Notch Mountain, waiting for the clouds to clear so that he could

---

1. Franklin Rhoda, "Report on the Topography of the San Juan Country" in U. S. Geological and Geographical Survey of the Territories, Annual Report 1874 (Washington: Government Printing Office), pp. 451–496.

be the first to photograph and prove the existence of the Mount of the Holy Cross. Jackson's son Clarence wrote later:

> Cold mist swirled about him as he worked his way very cautiously up to Notch's naked crest. He felt at once afraid and excited, alone in a sea of cottony white. And then, through a sudden rift of the clouds, he stared out over the gorge at the Holy Cross. It was true.[2]

The coming of the railroads had the effect of bringing other scientists to Colorado in the 1870s in addition to the official surveyors. Hayden's friend Othniel C. Marsh, the Yale paleontologist, arrived to gather fossils for his book on the history of the territory's plant and animal life. The botanists Asa Gray and C. C. Parry climbed the Gilpin County peaks that carry their names. George Bird Grinnell, the naturalist, found his way over the Medicine Bows into North Park and then encouraged ranchers to move into that high and peaceful pasture.

It was all done in the name of scientific progress, but one group of people, the six bands of Colorado Utes scattered about the western slope, were far from sure that science would be progressive for them. Their fears should have increased when the *Atlas of Colorado* appeared, revealing to everybody the startling fact that more than half of the Colorado Rockies did not belong to the new state but to a handful of Utes. The response of the settlers to this revelation was a slogan—"The Utes must go"— pronounced faintly at first but rising in decibels to a statewide roar.

As Robert M. Ormes has written in his classic *Guide to the Colorado Mountains,* the Utes were the true mountain people, "the dwellers of the turquoise sky," as they translate their tribal name. Their number in the 1870s was small—perhaps 3,500 all told. As early as the seventeenth century they had begun riding horses, acquired from the Spanish on the Rio Grande. At that

---

2. Clarence S. Jackson, *Picture Maker of the Old West* (New York: Charles Scribner's Sons, 1947), p. 189.

time the more "civilized" southerly Ute bands—Uncompahgres, Weminuches, Muaches, and Capotes—copied the
Pueblo Indians and the Navajos just south of them in raising
corn and beans, sheep and goats, along with their summer hunting for deer and elk in the mountains and for buffalo occasionally in the plains. The two northern groups—White River
and Grand River Utes—were more closely associated with the
Utes and Paiutes of Utah. The northern bands, on the whole,
were of a wilder, more independent temperament than the
southern bands.[3]

Through the 1859–1861 gold-rush period, the relations of the
Utes with the advancing whites were comparatively peaceful,
even friendly. The Utes were spared the pressures that drove the
Plains Indians to fierce resistance—pressures such as seizure of
their lands and destruction of the buffalo on which their way of
life depended. Ranch wives along the Front Range learned that
Utes passing by meant no harm when they demanded hot bis-
cuits or offered to trade a pony or two for one of the ranch
wives' children. Hordes of prospectors roamed through what the
Utes considered to be their private estate, but these invaders
kept mainly to the high country, which the Utes cared little
about because grass, water, and game were too scarce up there
for good hunting.

Still, conflict was bound to develop. To head it off, Governor
John Evans called to Denver in 1863 the nominal leader of the
six Ute bands, the multilingual Chief Ouray of the Uncompahgres. They concluded a treaty giving the Uncompahgres
possession "forever" of the Gunnison and Uncompahgre
river valleys. Five years later, Chief Ouray went to Denver
again to get specific land guarantees for all six of the Ute bands
from Governor Alexander C. Hunt. The result was one of the
most generous grants ever assigned to Indians by the U. S.

3. Robert M. Ormes, *Guide to the Colorado Mountains* (Denver: Sage Books, 1952),
p. 26.

COLORADO

A photographer's essay by Bob Peterson

Photographs in Sequence

State capitol at Denver.
Street in Leadville with Mount Massive in background.
Broadmoor Resort in Colorado Springs.
Town of Golden.
Main Street, Georgetown.
Independence Pass near Aspen.
Rafting on the Colorado River between Aspen and Glenwood Springs.
Gold mine near Malta.
Ghost-town buildings at Silver Plume.
Motorcyclist at Milner Pass in Rocky Mountain National Park.
Sloan Lake, Denver.
Mayflower Gulch in Arapaho National Forest.
Post office at Silver Plume.
Scene near Kremmling.
United States Air Force Academy glider near Pike's Peak.
Sailboats on Dillon Reservoir.

Senate—sixteen million acres "forever"—an area larger than Massachusetts, Connecticut, New Hampshire, and Rhode Island combined. This delectable oblong, 4,500 acres for each Ute man, woman, and child, was one hundred and ten miles from east to west, two hundred and twenty-eight miles from the border of New Mexico northward almost to Yampa River. It was bounded in the west by the Colorado-Utah border, in the east by the 107th meridian, which ran just west of the sites of present Aspen, Gunnison, and Gypsum.

The Senate's second grant of land "forever" turned out to last for five years. By 1873, the same irrepressible gold fever that created Colorado Territory in 1861 had propelled hundreds of prospectors up the Rio Grande from San Luis Valley and over Stony Pass, where they staked claims on Ute property and began to plat the town of Silverton. Chief Ouray sent word to President Grant by way of Governor McCook begging for troops from Fort Garland to drive out the trespassers. Grant started to send troops but recalled them when congressmen reminded him that soldiers were not allowed to fire on taxpayers.

The upshot was the Brunot Treaty of 1873, made at Los Pinos Agency by Chief Ouray and Felix Brunot, head of the Board of Indian Commissioners. One of the two witnesses to the treaty signing was a tiny man in his thirties named Otto Mears, the official trader at Los Pinos. Mears, one of the first of many Jewish pioneers to make his fortune in the back country, had wandered to Colorado from the bleak steppes of Russia by way of San Francisco, and he had a set of plans ready to exploit the San Juan gold rush with a system of toll roads, maybe even railroads, serving the new camps. The other witness was Governor McCook's ex-bodyguard and relative by marriage, General Charles Adams, who was Indian agent at Los Pinos after his transfer from service at the White River Ute Agency.

By the Brunot Treaty, amending the Treaty of 1868, Chief Ouray ceded to the United States four million acres of San Juan mineral lands in exchange for hunting privileges and annuities for the six bands to a value in livestock and farm equipment of $25,000 a year. We know now that the San Juan country would produce gold and silver worth a couple of hundred million dollars. That is why in hindsight we can forgive the Senate for its extravagance in doling out $15,000 more so that Ouray and his subchiefs could go East to marvel at the wonders of Washington and to enjoy in New York a special performance of the ballet-show, *The Black Crook*.

It was marked in Hayden's atlas of 1877 for all to see—a vast Ute Reservation, reduced a bit in 1873 but still containing twelve million acres. Obviously, the Utes must go. What right did that small group of ignorant savages have to those fertile valleys of the Gunnison and Grand, the White, Uncompahgre, Dolores, and the rest? It was deplorable that mining and making money did not interest them. All they cared about were their horses and their hunting. What could they do with those rich coal lands shown in the atlas in the Danforth Hills near the White River Agency? Or those priceless relics of prehistory, the cliff dwellings of Mesa Verde that they had kept secret for so long? The big problem was how to get the Utes out of Colorado without an uproar from the same misguided Indian lovers back East who had raised such a commotion over the Sand Creek affair. They had committed no atrocities, not even murdering settlers, as the Arapahoes had murdered the Hungate family in 1864. Hundreds of traders and Blake Street saloon keepers defended them because they were good customers. And that wily Chief Ouray—he was the biggest obstacle of all. He kept his bands in order and gave way just enough to white pressure to preserve the better part of the Ute estate.

But a crisis to solve the impasse was developing. In the spring of 1877 a tent-and-shack settlement popped up not far from the Ute Reservation so haphazardly that nine months passed before it got a name—Leadville. It adjoined two gloomy piles of rock to be called Fryer Hill and Carbonate Hill three

miles down California Gulch from Oro City. The Ute reservation began just over the Continental Divide to the west, less
than forty miles away. Leadvillé was not much to look at—a
bleak spot at 10,152 feet above sea level where snow was common in July and dynamite was used to dig graves in the per-
mafrost. Yet to thousands Leadville came to be beautiful. The
incredible richness of its silver mines, surpassing that of Nevada's Comstock Lode, would make it the second largest city in
the state within two years and the greatest single factor in the
growth of Colorado up to then—greater than the 1859 gold rush
or the boost which the Hill smelter gave to mining or the arrival
of railroads.

And the leader of the Leadville boom, its dynamic core,
was—of all people—the forty-six-year-old storekeeper with the
drooping handlebar moustache, Horace A. W. Tabor, whom we
saw last in Oro City apathetically celebrating statehood and
wondering why success had escaped him during his eighteen
years in Colorado. It has been told how Tabor and his antiseptic
wife, Augusta, moved their dying store business from Oro City
to the shack-town under Fryer Hill and found themselves, by the
spring of 1878, grossing a thousand dollars a day. "If," the no
longer apathetic Tabor announced in newspaper ads, "you want
anything from a small-sized needle to a large-sized elephant,
come and see me." [4] In addition to acquiring a modest affluence, Tabor had been elected mayor of Leadville and treasurer
of Lake County during the winter of 1878.

A phenomenon could be described as a series of extraordinary
coincidences producing miraculous results. The phenomenon of
Horace Tabor began on April 20, 1878, when a shoemaker
named August Rische and his companion George Hook trudged
over Mosquito Pass from Fairplay, where they had been trying
to learn how to tell ore from rock. They stopped at the Tabor

4. Duane A. Smith, *Horace Tabor* (Boulder, Colorado: Colorado Associated University Press, 1973), p. 61.

store in Leadville, received from the kindly and popular mayor a basket of groceries in exchange for a third interest in whatever they found as miners, walked up Fryer Hill, and began to dig. Eight days later, at a depth of twenty-seven feet, they hit a rich vein of silver carbonate. They called their strike the Little Pittsburg, and it became during its brief career one of the most famous lodes in the history of silver-mining.

In a few months, George Hook sold his third interest in the bonanza to Tabor and Rische for one hundred thousand dollars. As word of the mine's richness leaked out, a pack of lawyers began suits alleging that Tabor's vein surfaced in other claims, infringing the law of apex. Tabor had watched such suits for two decades and knew what to do. The Little Pittsburg was earning eight thousand dollars every day, and he could afford to buy out the claimants. As a further safeguard, Tabor and Rische paid Senator Jerome Chaffee $125,000 for his half interest in another Fryer Hill bonanza, the New Discovery. A bit later Chaffee bought out Rische, which led to a combine of Chaffee, Tabor, and David Moffat in a firm owning most of Fryer Hill, called the Little Pittsburg Consolidated Mining Company.

A feature of the phenomenon of Tabor in this period was his management skill under enormous pressure. He accepted his sudden imperial status calmly, switching from penny profits in the sale of "needles and elephants" to the handling of sums large enough to buy much of Colorado. His shambling, apologetic style did not change when he found himself to be the largest single stockholder of Chaffee's First National Bank of Denver—which meant, in effect, that he had become the state's top financier. He remained diffident when he was elected the Republican lieutenant governor of the state, an honor which he deserved because he had raised Leadville from infancy, and his child had grown so fast that it came to hold the balance of political power in the Republican party of Colorado.

In essence, a mining boom is a proliferation of confidence arising from the yearning of a host of people to get filthy rich in a hurry. Fryer Hill and Carbonate Hill were mere dots on the earth's surface—a few thousand acres of ground which were soon staked out. Those who came too late to find a claim had perfect confidence that they would discover another Little Pittsburg elsewhere in the region. The results of their searches were dozens of boom camps across the Continental Divide including Aspen, Ashcroft, and White Pine, just outside the presumed position of the east boundary of the Ute Reservation. Those who arrived late at these new diggings kept right on going west into Ute country to stake ground that would become Crested Butte and Irwin, Ruby and Gothic.

The Utes objected to these trespassers—mildly at first, and then furiously. Their reaction delighted the main promoter of the "the Utes must go!" slogan, the *Denver Tribune* reporter William B. Vickers, who had been looking for reasons to exterminate the Utes for years. As the Leadville boom expanded, Vickers filled the columns of the *Tribune* with slanted tales of Ute misconduct—how they were stealing horses and burros and tools from the miners, starting forest fires near the diggings, and misrepresenting the whereabouts of the reservation boundary. He neglected to report that posses of armed miners were invading Ute camps without legal authority and that some posse members made sexual overtures to Ute women, whose reputation for chastity was a part of Ute tradition. Vickers did not explain, either, that lightning was a common cause of fires in times of summer drouth. The biggest boost to his "Utes must go!" propaganda occurred on September 3, 1878, when a Middle Park rancher Old Man Elliott was allegedly shot to death while chopping wood, by a White River subchief with Uncompahgre connections, Chief Piah.

In the meantime, tensions of an entirely different kind were mounting between Utes and whites elsewhere. Nathan Cook Meeker, that admirable advocate of high standards in the conduct of human affairs, had been deprived of his position as

leader of Union Colony at Greeley. Some colony members objected to his temperance views, and some accused him of being
an atheist. When he defended his old friend William Byers during the Hattie Sancomb scandal, Greeleyites charged Meeker
with favoring free love. It was a bad time for him to lose his
job. At the age of sixty he was deeply in debt to the estate of the
late Horace Greeley, and he sank into despair during the months
that he spent trying to find respectable work.

And then, out of the blue sky, word came that Senator
Henry M. Teller had arranged his appointment by the Indian
Bureau as agent at the White River Ute Agency. In an instant
despair left him, and he was the Meeker of old—handsome,
trim, authoritative, jauntily confident and bursting with good in-
tentions. As he boarded the train on May 3, 1878, bound for
White River by way of Rawlins, Wyoming, he was once again
the romantic youth who had written novels about lifting savages
out of their misery. His mind swirled with plans for a model Ute
farm—the same sort of kindly plans that Europeans and Americans had pushed for three centuries—based on the belief that Indians could be made to think and behave like white men and
thus achieve the white man's spiritual joy and material benefits.
It was as inconceivable to Meeker as to those before him that
savages might prefer their own way of life—living in harmony
with their environment—to the white man's way of conquering,
sometimes destroying, his environment with the help of those
products of his ingenuity, steel plows, windmills, barbed wire,
sawmills, proper homes with stoves, privies, bathtubs, and all
the other marvels.

The White River Ute Agency was in a small meadow called
Agency Park on the river just above the site of present Meeker,
Colorado. It was some two hundred miles south of Rawlins and
Fort Steele, which was the post set up by the army to protect the
Union Pacific and the region around it from Indian attack. The
main White River Ute village was twelve miles downstream
from Agency Park in a broad and fertile bottom called Powell

Park, honoring John Wesley Powell, who had studied the Ute
language there in 1869 under the tutelage of the nominal leader
of the band, the aging and wispy Chief Douglas.

Meeker brought to White River a devoted staff of young people from Greeley. His wife, Arvilla, now a frail, anxious
woman of sixty-two, was the agency postmistress. Meeker's
daughter Josie, a gentle and beautiful girl of twenty-one, ran the
Ute school and agency boardinghouse. Among those instructing
the Utes in farming and ditch digging for irrigation was Shadrach Price. Shadrach's wife, Flora Ellen, full blown at sixteen
and the mother of two children, helped Josie with the boardinghouse. Another farming instructor was a sunny, curly-haired
teenager named Frank Dresser, who was so homesick for Greeley at first that he wrote a letter to his mother every day.

The new agent decided at once to move his operation to
Powell Park. It was far superior to Agency Park as a site for his
model Ute farm. Through the months ahead he and his staff
struggled against bewildering adversity to put into practice his
elaborate program for Ute salvation. Many Utes refused to stop
hunting for food and for elk hides, which they traded for guns
and ammunition. Meeker could not deny that they had reason to
hunt that winter of 1878–1879. Their annuity flour supplied by
the Indian Bureau was spoiling in Rawlins because the contractor had left town without paying the Union Pacific freight bill
and the railroad would not release it. Chief Douglas was inclined to co-operate with Meeker, but he was opposed by a
much younger man Chief Jack, who was intriguing to replace
him as head of the band.

Chief Douglas was opposed also by his medicine man Johnson, a superb horseman whose squaw was Chief Ouray's sister,
and by a big, blowzy subchief Colorow. This Colorow had two
grievances against the whites: General Adams had thrown him
out of Governor McCook's office in Denver a decade back; and
William Byers had banned him from taking his rheumatism cure
in the hot sulphur springs in Middle Park, which Byers was

improving for resort purposes. Meeker found germs of conflict even in his own family. Josie was smoking cigarettes and playing Spanish monte with the squaws. She seemed to be more interested in learning the ways of the Utes than in teaching the Utes the ways of the whites. And he wondered about her obvious affection for one of her pupils—not a child but a handsome twenty-six-year-old Indian named Persune, who had two squaws.

Added to these local symptoms of unrest was the general resentment of all the Utes in reaction to the "Utes must go!" campaign in the *Denver Tribune,* and the unsubtle editorials by William Vickers, hinting that it was wrong to teach Utes how to farm because they would then come in competition with white farmers. But Meeker's biggest problem was the love of the Utes for their thousands of ponies. The most fertile bottomland for farming lay in the pastures where these ponies had always grazed. As the medicine man Johnson explained it, many ponies were bred for racing, and they needed rich grass to run well. If these racers ran badly, rival ponies from Chief Ouray's Uncompahgre band would outrun them on the race track at Powell Park.

For months, Meeker treated Johnson with patience and courtesy, pointing out that the Utes could not become wealthy farmers, buy fine homes, and educate their children if they sacrificed their most productive croplands to feed all those useless ponies. But late in August 1879, Meeker's patience ran out when he discovered that Johnson was stealing Josie's schoolhouse water for his ponies. In a moment of frustration and rage, the agent ordered Shadrach Price to start plowing a new tract of pasture in Powell Park on which to plant two hundred acres of winter wheat. After some hours of plowing, Price heard bullets whining a few feet over his head. The warning bullets were being sent his way by several young Utes on the bench above the river. Price stopped plowing and reported the matter to Meeker.

Next morning, as Meeker was writing a long letter of complaint to the Indian Bureau in Washington, Johnson came into his office and asked the agent why Price was plowing up so much pony pasture. Meeker replied, "The trouble is this, Johnson. You have too many ponies. You had better kill some of them." For a long moment, Johnson, a tall, powerful man, did not move. Then he charged forward, picked up Meeker like a shock of corn, carried him outside, flung him hard against the hitching rail, and walked away without a word. Meeker was bruised but not seriously hurt. After some hours of indecision, he sent a courier to the telegraph office at Rawlins with a message to Carl Schurz, the secretary of the Interior, asking for troops to protect the agency staff.[5]

This message would bring on the second great interracial tragedy to occur in Colorado in fifteen years. On September 22, three companies of cavalry from Fort Steele—153 soldiers and twenty-five civilians—left Rawlins for White River under the command of Major Thomas T. Thornburgh. The men were merry in the golden crispness of that early autumn. To them this was a picnic into the mountains away from their drab station in the Wyoming desert. They did not think of the Utes as hostile Indians like the Sioux or Cheyennes. During noon rest a few days later, Chief Jack called on Thornburgh to complain that no troops were needed at the agency and to ask that the soldiers return to Fort Steele. Thornburgh told Jack that the troops would go no farther than the Milk Creek boundary of the Ute reservation while the major and five of his officers rode on to Powell Park to see what was bothering Meeker.

But the long cavalry column did not stop at Milk Creek on the morning of September 29. A hundred or so of Jack's followers watched from the ridge above as the troops began cross-

5. Robert Emmitt, *The Last War Trail* (Norman: University of Oklahoma Press, 1954), pp. 151–156. See also the account of the Milk Creek massacre in Marshall Sprague, *Massacre* (Boston: Little, Brown and Co., 1957), pp. 229–238.

ing the creek into the reservation. One of Thornburgh's soldiers spotted the Indians, and then a rifle cracked somewhere—a Ute rifle, or a soldier's. Major Thornburgh, a tall, lithe West Pointer in his thirty-fifth year, trotted forward calmly in the open to see what was up. In an instant he was dead and toppling from his horse as a hail of shots followed the first shot. During the next hour or so of battle, ten more soldiers were killed and twenty wounded before the troops could begin to barricade themselves behind wagons and dead mules. The ambush of Utes held them in that pastoral hollow until they were reinforced four days later by a company of Negro soldiers who had been on guard duty in Middle Park.

This black Company D was a unit of the Ninth Cavalry, one of six Negro regiments which the U. S. Army permitted itself reluctantly to recruit after the Civil War. Company D's white officer, a New Englander named Captain Francis S. Dodge, had one ambition—to lead his blacks into the sort of crisis that would show their fighting skill and courage for the education of white Americans who denied that blacks could fight. The superb performance of Company D in its rapid march west from Middle Park and its rescue of Thornburgh's white soldiers at Milk Creek was a triumph for Dodge and a turning point nationally along the rocky road to better relations between the two races.

Even before the battle between Thornburgh's men and the Utes began at Milk Creek, Chief Jack had sent a courier galloping off twenty-five miles to tell Douglas at the agency that Thornburgh had broken his word about stopping the troops at the reservation boundary. The courier found Douglas outside his tepee early in the afternoon. Up to then, the tension at Powell Park had been subsiding since word had come that Thornburgh would ride in to see Meeker without his soldiers. Frank Dresser, Shadrach Price, and other white employees were throwing up dirt to roof a new storehouse. Meeker was in his office reading Samuel Pepys's *Diary*. Arvilla Meeker, Josie, and the

housegirl, Flora Ellen Price, were in the Meeker kitchen clean-
ing up after lunch.

Jack's courier gave news of the battle to Douglas, who relayed it to several armed subchiefs gathered around him. There
was no discussion. The Utes walked slowly toward the new
storehouse, raised their guns, and began firing. Meeker ran out
of his office and fell with a bullet in his head. Within an hour
ten more male employees had been murdered—every white man
except Frank Dresser, who slipped away, badly wounded, to try
to reach Thornburgh's troops. Burning and looting followed. By
nightfall, the moonlit headquarters of Meeker's model farm was
a charred and deserted ruin dotted by corpses. Douglas's men
took Arvilla, Josie, Flora Ellen, and her children along with
them as hostages as they fled south to a secret camp across
Grand (Colorado) River on Grand Mesa. Eleven days later rescue troops hurrying to Powell Park from Rawlins noticed a trail
of blood near the old Danforth coal mine. The trail led them to
the mine entrance and the dead body of a curly-haired teenager,
a coat folded under his head and rifle cocked and clasped in his
hand. On a timber above his head he had managed to scrawl a
message before he died: "Have been here twenty-one hours. All
killed at the agency. Send my money to my mother at Greeley.
Frank Dresser." [6]

And so the "Utes must go!" campaign reached its final phase
as a smashing success in convincing a multitude of whites that
this small tribe was a menace to society. After twenty-three
days in custody of the Utes on Grand Mesa, the three white
women were released to General Adams, who was led to their
camp as a result of negotiations conducted by Chief Ouray of
the Uncompahgres with the White River band. Arvilla, Flora

6. Thomas F. Dawson and F. J. V. Skiff, *The Ute War* (Denver: Tribune Publishing
House, 1879), pp. 54–55.

Ellen Price, and Josie told Adams later that they had been "out-raged" by Douglas, Johnson, and Persune respectively during their captivity but that they did not want to testify publicly about such indelicate experiences. Josie seemed inclined to forgive Persune, explaining to Adams that even his squaws had urged her to submit on the grounds that if he took her as his third squaw other Utes would not dare to molest her. The entire testimony of the women was suppressed by Secretary of the Interior Schurz, who feared their charges that they had been raped by their captors might bring another orgy of revenge—whites against Indians—such as had occurred at Sand Creek in 1864.

After long federal hearings to decide who killed whom at Powell Park, Chief Douglas alone was judged criminal enough to be sent to prison at Fort Leavenworth, from which he was released in a year because no word was received from higher authority as to what he had done wrong. In June 1880, the Senate passed a bill causing the removal of Ouray's Uncompahgres and the White River bands to bleak lands nobody else wanted on the Green and Duchesne rivers in Utah. The Muache, Capote, and Weminuche bands fared better, having had no part in the White River massacre. They were assigned to acreages in southwestern Colorado where some two thousand of them remain—the Southern Utes (Muaches and Capotes) on farmlands around their headquarters town of Ignacio, and the Ute Mountain Utes (Weminuches) on grazing lands adjoining Mesa Verde National Park. Chief Ouray, who had struggled for twenty years to hold back the inexorable pressure of ever-increasing hordes of land-hungry whites, died at the age of forty-seven of Bright's disease, and perhaps of a broken heart, soon after the removal bill passed the Senate. Since then, as if in penitence for shabby tactics to drive the Utes to misbehavior, Coloradans have made Ouray a state hero, applying his name to the shapely peak just south of Monarch Pass, and the name of his wife Chipeta to a lesser summit near it. His portrait in stained glass is among those in the dome of the capitol in Denver.

Though Congress did not open the more than eleven million acres of vacated Ute lands to settlement until June 1882, homesteaders followed hard on the Utes as they withdrew to Utah in September 1881. From Gunnison town, hundreds of settlers rushed along Gunnison River and over Blue Mesa Summit (They called it "Son of a Bitch Hill.") and Cerro Summit just as Captain Gunnison had done in 1853 to get around the impassable Black Canyon of the Gunnison. As had happened in the gold rush of 1859, this new rush of settlers to the western slope included the usual American mix plus many immigrants from Europe—Swedes, Poles, Italians, Norwegians. And this time many of them brought their wives and children, since the civilization of the Front Range was not far away.

Before that year ended, some of these pioneers platted the town of Delta on the Gunnison at the mouth of the Uncompahgre. Others started a village at the junction of the Grand and Gunnison rivers that they would call Grand Junction in 1882. A group led by Joseph Selig laid out a town on the Uncompahgre near the site of what had been Chief Ouray's farm, calling it Ouray Junction at first and then Pomona, to suggest that it was the kind of place the Italian goddess of fruit and gardens would love. Selig disliked that name and persuaded his settlers to call it Montrose in tribute to Walter Scott's *The Legend of Montrose,* which he was reading at the time.

Samuel Wade and his friends moved around the north side of Black Canyon by way of Black Mesa to homestead the orchard country on the north fork of the Gunnison. Wade had brought some peony roots with him, and so his village was called Paonia. Meanwhile, ranchers flocked to the Yampa River valley just north of the old reservation boundary, and to the grasslands and dinosaur graveyards of the Little Snake River that Frémont had explored in 1844. The homestead of James Crawford became the town of Steamboat Springs, which had a gassy pool then that blew spray at ten-second intervals in the manner of the exhaust of a Mississippi stern-wheeler. The town of Meeker began in the fall of 1883 when the army removed the garrison that it had placed there soon after the Meeker massacre.

As the settlers rushed west, so did the railroads, whose builders had been held up by hard times and by the closed Ute reservation. Funds were easy to come by now. General Palmer's Denver and Rio Grande moved on from the railhead town of Alamosa (1878) in San Luis Valley over Cumbres Pass to his new supply town of Durango (1880), and on up the canyon of Animas River to Silverton. Here it connected to cliff-hanging stage roads built across the crest of the Rockies from Lake City and the mining camp of Ouray by the mighty midget of the San Juans, Otto Mears. Other Palmer branches got to Leadville (1880) through the Royal Gorge of the Arkansas and to Grand Junction (1882) by way of Marshall Pass and a dozen incredible miles through Black Canyon before Palmer's railroad master-piece was snatched from him by the refined piracy of Jay Gould. In this period, the narrow-gauge that W. A. H. Love-land had begun was serving Central City and Georgetown. John Evans, a reluctant associate of Jay Gould, built his Denver and South Park line across South Park and the Upper Arkansas Valley to reach Gunnison through the Alpine Tunnel under Alt-man's Pass.

All this expansion into what had been the secret wonderland of the Utes was not just a Colorado phenomenon. Its explosive dynamics derived primarily from the confidence and fascination of the whole world in the treasures of Leadville, with Horace Tabor and his Little Pittsburg mine as its glittering focus.

6

The County Makers
—and Cripple Creek

*W*HEN—long, long after the event—the opera *The Ballad of Baby Doe,* based on Tabor's scandalous love affair, had its premiere at the Central City Opera House in 1956, many older natives of the state were dismayed. It was disgraceful, they said, to make a hero of an adulterer.

But Douglas Moore, the composer, and John Latouche, the librettist, took a wider view. To them, Tabor was Everyman, with all the pathetic dreams of glory of the average male, who had advanced at the age of fifty-two from dreary subsistence and despairing nonentity to international fame, political power, sexual triumph, and inconceivable wealth. Through the 1880s, his story was relayed to the ends of the earth, and in such a way that Colorado seemed to be as much a part of his success as Tabor himself.

Though the Little Pittsburg bonanza was exhausted soon, Leadville's Croesus kept buying more Fryer Hill mines like the Matchless, and countless others along the Continental Divide— the Tam O'Shanter near Aspen, for instance, and several in the Park County and San Juan districts. It is probable that the value of the state as a whole owed much of its tenfold increase

101

through the 1880s to the stimulus provided by Tabor's compulsive buying as he scattered his own and borrowed millions on everything from gas and insurance companies to streetcar lines, ranches, irrigation ditches, toll roads, and uniforms for the Leadville police department. It is said that he spent $200,000 trying to become U. S. senator in 1883. The state legislature elected Thomas Bowen to the post, but Tabor was made a senator briefly—filling the thirty-day unexpired term of Henry Teller, who had resigned to become President Arthur's secretary of the Interior.

The popular appeal of this diffident creature with the drooping moustache was of the broadest kind. Whereas other Colorado kingpins like John Evans and General Palmer maintained themselves as models of propriety, Tabor went out of his way to show that he was both bad and good. He divorced the admirable but unappetizing Augusta in 1882 at a cost of $350,000 and took up with a ravishing divorcee from Wisconsin, described as "the Belle of Oshkosh" and "a Dresden doll" by her biographer Caroline Bancroft.[1] Her maiden name was Elizabeth McCourt, but she was called Baby Doe after her marriage in her teens to Harvey Doe. Baby Doe was small, blue-eyed, and possessed of a fetching plumpness when, at the age of twenty-eight, she met Tabor. She was neither a dance-hall girl nor a prostitute but one of a number of respectable young women who, after their marriages soured, popped up in Central City or in Leadville demurely on the prowl for a replacement spouse, preferably a bonanza king.

Tabor installed his mistress in Denver's new Windsor Hotel and married her at the Willard in Washington during his thirty days as senator. President Arthur was among the guests gasping at the most sumptuous nuptials that the nation's capital had ever seen. Tabor's gift to his bride was a $75,000 diamond necklace that was alleged to have been pawned by Queen Isabella of

1. Caroline Bancroft, *Silver Queen* (Denver: Golden Press, 1950), p. 6.

Spain in 1492 to finance the first voyage of Columbus to America. Later Tabor paid $54,000 (the equivalent of half a million today) for a Denver mansion at Thirteenth and Sherman, and the couple set up housekeeping while the town's elite ladies, the whist-playing "Sacred Thirty-Six," ignored them utterly, and talked of nothing else.

What nobody knew until Tabor went bankrupt during the Panic of 1893 was that this ignoble affair had a noble twist. The wicked old man and his gold-digging paramour had fallen deeply and permanently in love. After Tabor's death in 1899, his penniless widow, shorn even of Queen Isabella's jewels, remained faithful to his memory for thirty-six years by standing guard alone at his played-out Matchless Mine on Fryer Hill until her death by freezing and malnutrition in a shack near the shaft-house of the Matchless.

While legends grew about Tabor's lack of culture, he began using some of his wealth to help Denver emerge from the planless chaos of its pioneer days into a city of aesthetic distinction. As a first step he went East in 1879 and hired Chicago's best young architects, the brothers Frank and W. J. Edbrooke, to design an office building worthy of the city's new status as beneficiary of the treasure pouring out of Leadville. The resulting Tabor Block on Larimer Street was a sensation. When newsmen of the day called it "a Temple to Progress, worthy of any city in the world," they were inaugurating the custom of exalted hyperbole that Denverites have followed ever since. The Tabor Block cost $365,000, soared five stories, and was built of carved limestone, perhaps in honor of Tabor's work as a youthful stonemason back in Vermont. Before residents could catch their breath, Tabor and Frank Edbrooke were touring the East gathering ideas for a far greater project, the million-dollar Tabor Grand Opera House at Sixteenth and Curtis. It opened on September 5, 1881, to a first-night throng who came to hear the soprano Emma Abbott in the Irish opera *Maritana*.

Having been lured west by Tabor, Frank Edbrooke never left

Denver. He brought to the city what writer Richard Brettell has called "Denver's first truly civilized buildings," including the massive McPhee Block at 17th and Glenarm, the Chamber of Commerce headquarters at 14th and Lawrence, and the Metropole Hotel (today's Cosmopolitan). His masterpiece remains the triangular Brown Palace Hotel at 17th and Broadway, with its curved corners, intricate facade, and high-rise lobby. The owner was a wealthy contractor named Henry C. Brown, who had turned up in Denver with the rest of the early birds in 1860 and pre-empted a quarter section of bluffs at $1.25 an acre a mile and a half south of town. The Brown Palace had cost him the staggering sum of $1,600,000 by the time of its opening in 1892. It might have vanished long ago with the Windsor and other obsolete inns, but age has only increased its charm.[2]

Henry Brown, Horace Tabor, and Edbrooke had roles in another part of the state's architectural history. Martin Wenger, in his paper for the Denver Westerners *Brand Book of 1952,* explained how Brown deeded ten acres of his bluff to Colorado Territory back in 1868 to be used as a site for a badly needed territorial capitol building. When nothing was done about it even after statehood, Brown reclaimed what had come to be known as Capitol Hill and put a fence around it to discourage trespass by the state. Years of lawsuits ensued while five governors in succession tried to clear title to the hill and to raise money for a million-dollar statehouse. In 1885, five hundred of the nation's architects were asked to compete for the design of the capitol building. The winner was Elijah E. Myers of Detroit, who described his plans as "Greek Corinthian," though critics called them "modified Washington, D. C." Frank Edbrooke placed second in the contest with a design titled mysteriously "Simplex Munditiis." The U. S. Supreme Court meanwhile denied Brown's claim to the hill, and an Illinois man won the con-

2. Richard R. Brettell, *Historic Denver* (Denver: Historic Denver, Inc., 1973), p. 33.

struction contract, which specified that the capitol be built of granite from the Zugwelder quarry near Gunnison, with wainscotting of onyx from the Wet Mountains.[3]

Horace Tabor was in charge of the laying of the cornerstone on July 4, 1890. Fifteen thousand people were on hand for the parade, the mammoth barbecue, and the sealing of articles— Holy Bible, Denver City Directory, an 1811 edition of Zebulon Pike's *Journal,* and such—in the cornerstone. Judge Wilbur Stone declared that the capitol was "the crowning glory of the Queen City of the Centennial State. It will ever stand a monument to the bravery and endurance of the pioneers of 1859–1860." [4] The judge failed to mention Elijah Myers, the creator of this crowning glory, since he had been dismissed a year earlier on charges of trying to move his private debts to the state's public debit account.

With the cornerstone laid, construction dragged on and on, even after Frank Edbrooke was hired in 1898 to speed things up. It was Edbrooke's idea to enhance the capitol dome with sixteen window portraits in stained glass of the state's leading men—Gilpin, Evans, N. P. Hill, William Byers, General Palmer, and Chief Ouray among them, but, of course, no scandalous Horace Tabor. The building as it stands today was completed in 1908 at a total cost of $3,492,744.38. The final Edbrooke touch was to cover the dome with $4,000 worth of gold leaf, surmounted by a 1,400-candlepower incandescent globe.

Critics complain that the arbitrary straight-line boundaries of Colorado destroy regional harmony. They argue that the eastern plains should be in Kansas, the northwest in Wyoming, the

3. Martin Wenger, "Raising the Gold-Plated Dome," *Denver Westerners Brand Book, 1952* (Denver: Denver Westerners, 1953), p. 119.
4. Wenger, "Gold-Plated Dome," p. 125.

Colorado River drainage in Utah, while San Luis Valley and the southern watershed of the Arkansas should belong to New Mexico just as they did in the Spanish seventeenth century.

The critics have a point, if one prefers consistency to color and variety. Much of the excitement of the state's history derives from its crazy-quilt effect. After statehood a symptom of the trend toward diversity was the break up of Colorado into a welter of counties, each seeking to be independent and still a loyal though grumbling part of the whole. The gold rush of 1859 began in a single huge county, Arapahoe (Kansas Territory), and then Governor Gilpin's legislature reduced its size and laid out sixteen more counties, on the map at least, to give Colorado Territory an organized air. Two of these new counties, Lake and Summit, stretched all the way to Utah. Each of them was more than twice as large as Massachusetts. They were technically out of order, along with Conejos County in the southwest, since part of their areas lay within the private property of the Utes. Four of the new eastern counties—Weld, Arapahoe, Douglas, and Huerfano—ran from the Front Range to Kansas. In the 1870s these four eastern counties consisted largely of land in the public domain that had been appropriated free of charge by the cattle kings John W. Iliff, John W. Prowers, and a number of absentee Scotch and English investors.

As populous towns appeared around the new gold and silver camps, the resident miners found how easy it was to carve a county of their own out of one of the original seventeen, with a county seat conveniently close by to handle their legal affairs instead of hundreds of miles away. The Colorado constitution provided that this could be done by calling for a vote on the separation issue within the large county. Since the gold-silver communities were apt to have a majority of the population of the county, the proponents of separation usually got their way. If the issue was in doubt, they had funds to lobby in the state legislature and, as one old-timer put it, "they could register the votes of approving horses, cows, mules, goats, sheep, and chickens.'' Several new western counties and county seats were created in 1874, soon after the Utes released the San Juan mining districts—Hinsdale (with its county seat at Lake City), Rio Grande (Del Norte), San Juan (Silverton), and La Plata (Parrott City). A second orgy of western county carving resulted from the removal of the Utes in 1881—Garfield (Glenwood Springs), Eagle (Eagle), Pitkin (Aspen), Montrose (Montrose), Mesa (Grand Junction), and Rio Blanco (Meeker).

Meanwhile, only three new counties were formed on the semiarid eastern plains, which remained virtually empty of people through the 1870s except for those living in a few cattle-trail towns serving the open-range cattle industry along the Kansas Pacific and Santa Fe railroads. The Plains Indians were only an unhappy memory. They were seen no more in their old Colorado hunting grounds after roving bands of Cheyennes were defeated by soldiers in two battles—at Beecher Island near present Wray in 1868, and a year later at Summit Springs south of Sterling.

The tremendous increase of population and business enterprise after the Leadville boom forced the state out of its preoccupation with mining into a more rounded economy that would bring its most remote parts into use, including those empty eastern plains and sandhills that were thought of still as ''the great American desert.'' Coloradans had to eat, and the irrigated croplands along the South Platte and Arkansas were not meeting the demand for food. Dry-land farming—growing crops without irrigation—was an old idea, but it did not come to the plains on a large scale until the mid-1880s, when three railroads—Burlington, Rock Island, and Pueblo and State Line (Missouri Pacific)—headed for the Front Range cities from the east along the spring-fed courses of the Republican and Smoky Hill rivers.

To help pay the cost of building the three new lines across the Colorado plains, the railroad companies became ardent land developers. Their agents conducted campaigns among farmers of eastern Kansas and Nebraska urging them to increase their acreage and make estates for their children by moving to the dry lands of eastern Colorado served by the three railroads—to public lands which the government would give to them for practically nothing. The campaigns were highly successful; an American tradition was carried on. As the seaboard farmers of the eighteenth century had been lured over the Alleghenies to improve their fortunes in Ohio and Kentucky, and then over the Mississippi to Missouri and Oregon and California, so in the 1880s thousands of young Kansas and Nebraska families along with emigrant families from Russia and Germany piled their belongings into covered wagons and made for the Colorado frontier, driving their livestock before them.

These dry-land pioneers were quite different from the gold-rush Fifty-Niners, who had been motivated by greed for wealth and power. By contrast, the migrating farmers were impelled by simple pastoral dreams—of being their own boss, of matching wits with nature, of winning homes of their own on land of their own. But the railroad agents were careful not to prepare them for the reality of their Colorado Eden. The Homestead Act of 1862 limited a man to 160 free acres of prairie, which in Colorado had none of the productivity of the same acreage in the humid East. Under the Timber Culture Act of 1878—drawn by misguided Easterners who believed that trees would attract moisture and make the desert bloom—a second 160 acres could be acquired free if one planted ten acres of seedling trees, 2,700 trees per acre, and kept 675 of them alive for five years. Finally, if a farmer was lucky enough to possess $200, or was able to borrow it from a loan shark at fifteen-percent interest, he could enlarge his farm to 480 acres by pre-emption at $1.25 an acre. His problem then was to raise children and horses fast enough to provide labor and motive power to operate such a spread.

From 1885 on, the dry-landers poured into eastern Colorado, staked their homesteads, plowed up the sagebrush and buffalo grass, and prayed that their corn and wheat, barley and oats, would grow where crops had never grown before. They could not have picked a more opportune time for pioneering. They were spared serious conflict with the cattle kings, who knew by 1885 that their control of the open range was almost over. And a providential cycle of wet years had just begun, giving the farmers the illusion that they could count on at least twenty inches of annual rainfall as in the East. (The normal average for the high plains was less than nine inches.)

And still theirs was an epic struggle with few parallels in the nation's agricultural history. In this barren region at an altitude of four thousand feet above sea level every means of survival had to be invented on the spot. The last of the buffalo that had sustained the Plains Indians had been slaughtered by the hide and bone hunters. The supply of rabbit and antelope for food was not dependable. The staple diet at first was mush and milk. Water for livestock and household was a rare commodity. To get it, one had to haul it in barrels from a neighbor's well miles away, or dig for it by hand—a hundred and fifty feet or more down in the sandy loam. There were no roads—only the dim marks of wagon wheels. The occasional community square dance lasted until dawn so that people could see their wagon tracks and follow them home. There were no trees for lumber or firewood. Buffalo chips did for fuel. Houses were basement "dugouts," cut in a slope of prairie with windows just above ground, or structures of sod some twenty-four feet long by eighteen feet wide. The sod was cut with a plow in long slabs to make walls for the building that were three or four feet thick. The roofs of thick turf piled on boards leaked a bit, but nobody complained. The precious water was caught in pots and basins and saved for use. The inside walls of the earth house were plastered with a pink clay—"magnesia"—found in the banks of dry streambeds. Architecturally a "soddy" looked primitive, but it proved to be marvelously cool in summer and warm in winter.

By trial and error, heroic persistence, and ingenuity, the dry-land pioneers learned how to endure the terrors of their new home—tornadoes and blizzards, lightning, plagues of grasshoppers, rattlesnakes. The most heartbreaking of catastrophes were the summer hailstorms, destroying in five minutes a field of ripening grain—product of a full year of toiling and hoping. Dry weather threatened catastrophe too. Professional rainmakers were popular, particularly a tall and gaunt Australian named Frank Melbourne, who claimed to have caused downpours all over the world. His charge for rain was six cents an acre. His method was to burn incense in a loft of a barn while mumbling incantations to the heavens. He had a few successes, but usually, as one witness said, his rain would not quench the thirst of a grasshopper. It was found later that he picked his dates for raining from *Hicks's Almanac,* a St. Louis publication, which predicted everybody's weather for five years ahead.

Through all their trials, the Colorado dry-landers enjoyed good health. Doctors were few and very far between. Wives were superbly durable and delivered amazing quantities of children without professional help. Illnesses at home were cured by Castoria and castor oil and mustard plaster. Turpentine was the favored antiseptic. A poultice of tobacco quids was good for snakebites. Matted cobwebs stopped bleeding. The weather was surprisingly agreeable. Though the winters could be severe for brief periods, the springs and falls were glorious, and even the heat of summer was pleasant in that dry atmosphere. Some newcomers were shocked by the bleakness of the prairie. But they found beauty in it later as they came to feel themselves a part of the grandeur of earth and sky.

As the farmers staked their homesteads, the railroad townsites filled magically. The first lots in Holyoke on Frenchman Creek were sold at auction on September 21, 1887. Two weeks later forty-two buildings were going up. The town of Wray, south of the sandhills in Arikaree Valley, blossomed in the same year, and so did Yuma and Akron west of Wray. The Rock Island sponsored Burlington and Flagler. Cheyenne Wells and Kit Carson were pets of the Kansas Pacific on the old Smoky Hill Trail between Kansas City and Denver. Eads was backed by the Pueblo and State Line Railroad. Lamar and Granada were Santa Fe promotions. Still farther south, Springfield was begun on the promise of being served by a branch of the Santa Fe that did not arrive until 1926. Most of these towns were given names that had no relation to Colorado or its people. They were picked by railroad officials with sentimental memories of ther hometowns back East. The name ''Flagler'' honored Henry M. Flagler, the Florida rail tycoon. Lamar was named for President Cleveland's secretary of the Interior, Lucius Q. W. Lamar, in exchange for giving the place a government land office.

The infant towns agreed at once on the first order of business—to break away from that handful of monster eastern counties, the seats of which were in distant Front Range cities. These counties had been kept intact through the lobbying in the capitol at Denver of the cattle kings, who didn't mind county governments that confined themselves to Front Range affairs but wanted no politicians meddling with their feudal domain out in the plains. But the anticounty slush fund of the cattlemen was puny by the mid-1880s. The dry-land farmers became as adept at counting the votes of their domestic animals as the miners had been some years earlier. Residents of Akron started the county making on February 9, 1887, when the legislature allowed them to detach for themselves a large chunk of Weld County under the name of Washington County. Sixteen days later, another chunk of Weld became Logan County, with Sterling as the county seat. A lull followed, and then came the deluge of 1889 as the Seventh General ''County-Making'' Assembly demolished the old county setup with thirteen new eastern counties pretty much as they stand today.

It was a fortunate development. Four years later, the deceptive cycle of wet years ended, and four years of drouth settled over the Colorado plains. Nearly all the crops which the dry-landers had been growing by Eastern methods withered and died and blew away. Pre-emption debts could not be paid or loans extended because of the Panic of 1893. A mass exodus of pioneer families ensued. Homesteads were abandoned or traded for something useful—a pistol or a sewing machine or a churn. All that held the region together was the legal business of the new county seats and the funds to maintain their buildings and employees, which came mainly from tax money paid by the railroads.

And yet a stubborn, hardy remnant of dry-landers hung on through every crisis of bankruptcy and desperation. Groups of them made a habit of meeting to discuss their problems and exchange information about drouth-resisting crops and ways of planting and cultivating to preserve moisture. Some gave up crops and turned to raising cattle on the grasses that had done so well by the buffalo. There was a good deal of shifting to more promising homesteads. And when the drouth finally eased in 1896, these diehard farmers found themselves possessed of experience that they had lacked in the beginning. Crop yields and land values began a slow but steady rise, and their old optimism returned.

More hard times were ahead for them, but they had won a major victory over this demanding land that they had come to love as much for its perennial challenge as for its evanescent beauty.

During the middle 1880s Senator Henry M. Teller and other Coloradans perceived that the huge production of silver of Leadville and its neighbors foreshadowed a disaster that could wreck the economy of the mountain west. So much silver was being thrown on world markets that its value was declining. That made it unstable as a medium of exchange in partnership with gold at the traditional ratio of sixteen ounces of silver to one of gold. By his astuteness and forthrightness, Teller had become a power in the Republican party and the leading proponent of bimetallism—that is, the unlimited coinage of both silver and gold. Teller's arch foe was President Cleveland, who persuaded Congress in 1893 to stop buying silver at its fixed ratio and to put the country on the single gold standard. Cleveland argued that the financial panic spreading from Europe to the United States was caused partly because the Treasury Department had to pay more for silver than it was worth to meet the limited commitment of the Sherman Silver Purchase Act of 1890.

Repeal of the Purchase Act had a catastrophic effect in Colorado which had led the nation in silver production for a decade. Thousands lost their jobs as every silver mine and smelter was forced to shut down. Banks closed, railroads stopped hauling ore, and terrorism broke out as desperate men turned to violence to get food for their families. In the fall of 1892, the voters backed the new and radical Populist Party because it stood for bimetallism, while the Democrats and Republicans shillied and shallied. Populism was a midwestern movement with a platform calling for lower freight rates and higher crop prices for farmers among other reforms that seemed drastic then—reforms like the graduated income tax, eight-hour day, and direct election of senators. Though Populism got nowhere nationally, it triumphed in Colorado when its candidate for governor, an Aspen newspaper editor named Davis H. Waite, won the election.

Waite, a brave and earnest firebrand on the order of the Kansas abolitionist John Brown, was a blunt man. In a speech against the gold standard before a crowd of silver people in Denver, he declared:

> Our weapons are argument and the ballot. And if the money power shall attempt to sustain the usurpations by the strong hand, we will meet that issue when it is forced upon us, for it is better, infinitely better, that blood should flow to the horses' bridles rather than our national liberties should be destroyed.[5]

5. Fritz, *Colorado*, p. 354.

The New Testament phrase about the horses' bridles was from Revelations 15, and Waite was implying a parallel between "the money power" and the "idolators" in the Bible whom the pure in heart were battling. His seeming demand for revolutionary action frightened the state's conservatives out of their wits. Also it brought upon the orator the derisive nickname, "Bloody Bridles" Waite—enough in itself to limit his political career to those two short years as governor.

Waite's views were ahead of his time but his election was instructive to Senator Teller. It confirmed Teller's belief that he could not go on being a Republican and a bimetallist at the same time—a belief that produced one of the great dramatic moments of American politics. It came in 1896 during the national Republican convention in St. Louis, which Teller attended with the Colorado delegation. He was aged sixty-six now, a frail old man suffering from asthma. As expected, a gold-standard plank was read, and Teller took the floor to present a substitute motion for free coinage. It had no chance. The audience knew that Teller's motion amounted to his farewell address. His biographer Elmer Ellis quoted his remarks in part:

> When the Republican party was organized, I was there. It has never had a national candidate since it was organized that my voice has not been raised in his support. . . . With its great leaders, its distinguished men of forty years I have been in close communion and with many of them on terms of close friendship. I have shared its honors and its few defeats. Yet I cannot before my country and my God, agree to that provision that shall put upon this country a gold standard and I will not. I do not care what may be the result. If it takes me out of political life, I will go out with a feeling that at least I have maintained my consistency and my manhood, and that my conscience is clear and that my country will have no right to find fault with me. . . . As a bimetallist I must renounce my allegiance to my party.[6]

6. Elmer Ellis, *Henry Moore Teller* (Caldwell, Idaho: The Caxton Printers, 1941), p. 260.

When the senator finished speaking, the convention adopted the gold plank by a huge majority. Then Teller got to his feet on the platform and so did the youthful Senator Cannon of Utah. Arm in arm, the two of them strolled down the aisle and out of the hall, followed by the entire Colorado and Idaho delegations and by delegates from other mining states—twenty-three delegates in all.

Within minutes, news of the bolt reached the cities of Colorado by telegraph. A wild, statewide celebration began with impromptu bands parading, bonfires burning and cannon booming on both sides of the Continental Divide. Later Teller and the rest of the bolters formed the Silver Republican Party. Their support enabled William Jennings Bryan to win the Democratic nomination for president in 1896 on a bimetallist platform that, Bryan said a thousand times, was intended to prevent the Republican candidate, William McKinley, from "crucifying mankind on a cross of gold."

While battle lines were drawn for the bitterest presidential campaign since the Civil War, a paradox was developing on the other side of Pikes Peak from Colorado Springs, General Palmer's effete resort for the idle rich. Back East in 1859, that mountain landmark had been regarded as central to the gold rush. But no gold was ever discovered on Pikes Peak in those early years by the countless prospectors who had picked it over inch by inch. Mining experts agreed that none ever would be. But an amiable Springs cowboy, Bob Womack, claimed that gold is where you find it, not where it is supposed to be. From 1870 on, he had been telling friends that he would find it at the head of a tiny Pikes Peak stream called Cripple Creek, where his cattle sometimes lamed themselves trying to cross the steep banks. And in the fall of 1890 he did find his El Paso Lode. Nobody believed him until spring, when a few gullible men rode their horses in from the Colorado Midland railroad station at nearby Florissant and began scratching on the round hills of

Bob's summer cow pasture, which was not really Bob's land but part of the unclaimed public domain.

Womack's discovery made him famous at Cripple Creek in time but did little else for him. He was the kind of prospector who enjoyed looking for gold more than finding it. After striking the rich El Paso Lode, he lost interest in it soon and sold his share for three hundred dollars. One of his friends up there was not so careless. Winfield Scott Stratton was a first-rate carpenter who had been earning three dollars a day through the 1880s building huge chateau and shingle-style homes and stables in the north end of Colorado Springs, where most of the nabobs lived. Stratton was a sort of bachelor. He had married a seventeen-year-old girl in 1876 but called the marriage off when his bride confessed that she was pregnant by someone else. Thereafter he spent his spare time prospecting wherever gold and silver were found—Leadville, Aspen, the San Juans, Kokomo, Redcliff, Tincup. He studied geology and assaying at Colorado College. When Womack took him up to Cripple Creek to look at the place, he probably knew as much about precious-metal mining in the Rockies as any man alive.

Stratton knew, for instance, from F. V. Hayden's *Atlas of Colorado,* that Bob's cow pasture was the site of an extinct volcano. For weeks he poked around telling the tenderfeet that the camp was a dud. Then, on July 4, 1891, he staked a granite ledge at the foot of Battle Mountain and put the name "Independence" on his location notice. He had recognized that the ledge was on the rim of Hayden's volcano. Eight years later, when his total net profit in gold taken from the Independence came to more than six million dollars, he sold it to an English company for eleven million dollars—the highest price ever paid to one man for one mine. By then, the world knew that Bob's cow pasture was the richest ten thousand acres that had ever been discovered, with gold production that would reach a value of half a billion dollars.

Stratton's fortune in the 1890s was twice as large as Horace

Tabor's had been in the 1880s. The contrast between the two was evident from the way each of them spent his money. Tabor was gregarious, loving, confident, careless, and happy. Money to him was something to be spewed out on ostentatious living. Stratton was a loner, unattractive, suspicious, neurotic. He had no use for the things that multimillionaires liked to buy—not women or castles in Spain or yachts or jewels. His only interest was in finding mines, not striking it rich. Though he invested some of his wealth in Colorado real estate including a mortgage on the Brown Palace Hotel in Denver, he put most of it back into Cripple Creek in search of the volcanic mother lode where all the veins came together. He never found it, and he might have gone broke trying if he had not died of alcoholism, aged fifty-four, in 1902. He had several millions left. His will assigned his estate to trustees for the establishment of a sanctuary for indigent children and old people, the Myron Stratton Home, which thrives still in Colorado Springs.

The paradox of Cripple Creek lay in the timing. As silver lost value and the state's silver mines went bankrupt, gold appreciated, causing commodity prices to fall, interest rates to rise, and bringing misery to debtors who had to pay their debts with dollars that were worth more than the dollars they had borrowed. Stratton was envied everywhere because each day's deflation made him richer in gold. Stratton himself was not pleased. During the Bryan-McKinley contest, while people wondered what princely sum he would give in support of the gold-standard Republicans, the incredible news came that he was backing William Jennings Bryan and silver. Stranger still, he put up a hundred thousand dollars in cash to be bet on a Bryan victory if someone would bet $300,000 on McKinley. (Though McKinley's election was regarded as a sure thing, the bet was not covered.) In a statement to reporters, Stratton said:

I do not make the offer because of any information that I have on the election, but I have a feeling that Bryan is going to win. I am

deeply interested in seeing Bryan elected. I realize that the
maintenance of the gold standard would perhaps be best for me
individually, but I believe that free silver is the best thing for the
working masses of this country.[7]

The story of all that gold from Bob Womack's cow pasture
reached its peak of paradox in the decline of Bryan's political
fortune after the election of McKinley in 1896. Cripple Creek
gold increased the world supply so much that the metal began to
lose value, just as silver had done in the 1880s. As a result, that
shining knight of the underprivileged, Bryan, lost his "Cross of
Gold" appeal and was beaten by McKinley a second time in
1900. And by 1908, when Bryan suffered his third and final
defeat, bimetallism was a dead issue.

7. Frank Waters, *Midas of the Rockies* (New York: Covici-Friede, 1937), p. 169.

7

Colorado Goes Federal

$\mathcal{U}$NTIL World War II, the men who determined the development of Colorado were residents of the state—with one notable exception.

Theodore Roosevelt was forty-one years old in September 1900, when he visited the state for the first time as Republican nominee for vice-president under William McKinley. Roosevelt combined an objective knowledge of his country and its history with the instincts of a party politician, and he had an extraordinary magnetism. People who looked at that great head and those gleaming teeth above his stocky frame, cheered themselves hoarse whether they believed what he was saying or not.

Roosevelt's interest in Colorado derived partly from his conviction that the unoccupied public domain of the mountain west—its forests, its wildlife, the headwaters of its rivers—should be conserved for the benefit of all Americans and not just for the benefit of the states enclosing them. His passionate love of the outdoors and its pleasures—especially hunting—derived from the struggle of his youth to overcome the handicap of a frail, asthmatic body. Three years of that successful struggle—1883–1886—were spent on his Elkhorn and Maltese Cross cattle ranches in North Dakota, the problems of which made him a disciple of the famous John Wesley Powell, explorer of the

Grand Canyon. Powell had been arguing for years that the West would remain the "great American desert" unless the federal government began a program of reclamation by large-scale irrigation using water from watersheds protected by national forest reserves.

Conservation remained one of Roosevelt's major interests when he returned from North Dakota to New York to serve his party as a New York City police reformer, as McKinley's assistant secretary of the navy in 1896, as leader of the Rough Riders in the Spanish-American War, and as Republican governor of New York. At Albany, he applied some conservationist principles to the Adirondacks, but his tendencies toward reform did not please Thomas C. Platt, the Republican boss of the state, who put him out of action in 1900 by arranging his nomination as vice-president for McKinley's second term. The prospect of four years under the thumbs of McKinley and his big-business friends was sickening for Roosevelt. As vice-presidential nominee, however, he found a kindred spirit in a young forest-bureau expert in the Department of Agriculture named Gifford Pinchot who was even more fanatical about conservation than he was.

At that time Pinchot was taking note of what was happening to some forty-two forest reserves, the first of which had been set up by President Benjamin Harrison in 1891. These western reserves totaled forty-five million acres of public domain unclaimed by homesteaders. Four were in Colorado, including the White River Plateau Timber Reserve, a million-acre tract in the beautiful Flattop country around Trappers Lake that had been a favorite hunting ground of the Ute Indians. It was the nation's second forest reserve, proclaimed on October 16, 1891, by President Harrison soon after he set up the Yellowstone Park Timber Land Reserve in Wyoming.

The reserves were established to control overgrazing by a system of livestock permits and to save snow water needed for irrigation by preventing lumber companies from cutting down trees in the high country. Pinchot told Roosevelt that these aims were being defeated in Colorado because the Silver Republican Senator Henry Teller and the gold-standard Republican Senator Edward O. Wolcott had blocked the appropriation of funds to pay for qualified personnel to enforce the rules of the reserves. The lumbermen and stockmen of Routt County had convinced the senators that the creation of the White River reserve was an invasion of state's rights, that the reserve was retarding settlement, and that most of it was not forest anyhow, but sage and scrub oak.

When Roosevelt came to Denver in September 1900 to campaign for McKinley, he remembered hearing that some Coloradans favored the White River reserve, including several wealthy sportsmen from Colorado Springs who had been going to White River to hunt ever since the removal of the Utes. One of these hunters, Philip B. Stewart, had attended Yale with Roosevelt's family physician, Dr. Alexander Lambert, and had written to Lambert that the White River country abounded not only in deer and elk but in "cougars." To bag a mountain lion was one of Roosevelt's highest ambitions. He wired Stewart from Chicago, inviting him to join the campaign train in Colorado Springs and tell him about these cougars as they rode along.

Stewart was a liberal Republican with a good knowledge of Colorado's peculiar gold-versus-silver politics. Roosevelt felt at home with him because of their Ivy League backgrounds— Stewart had been Skull and Bones at Yale and captain of the baseball team that had whipped Harvard in 1886. Stewart told the vice-presidential nominee that the silver issue of William Jennings Bryan was alive in the state but waning. Roosevelt had his doubts about this when his train climbed up to the Cripple Creek mining district. A riot broke out as he and Senator Wolcott tried to address a crowd of Bryan supporters in the town of Victor. While beer bottles and furniture were flying around, somebody banged Roosevelt on the shoulder with a placard reading "Hang T. R." Roosevelt, who was extremely short-sighted, reached for the placard wielder, failed to locate him, and was heard to mutter, "Any goddamned man born with such eyes as I've got ought to have been knocked in the head in his cradle." As he was hustled out of Victor, Roosevelt was told that the miners were not really mad at him but at Senator Wolcott, who had reneged in 1896 on a promise to join the Silver Republicans.[1]

Bryan carried Colorado barely when McKinley was re-elected president in November, but the Victor riot won a good deal of sympathy for Roosevelt. He had not campaigned with much fervor, being preoccupied with plans for a Colorado cougar hunt in January with Phil Stewart. From his governor's desk back in Albany, he deluged Stewart with questions about White River. "Shall I bring my 30-30 Winchester? Will I need my revolver?" He asked Stewart to buy him proper hunting garb— chest 44, hips 42, shoes No. 7, hat size 7⅜. "I have a fur cap which draws down over the ears, just the thing for one of those scampering rides . . . My venerable buckskin shirt does not look well because I have swelled considerably since I used to wear it seventeen years ago." Late in December his anticipation became unbearable. "Upon my word," he wrote Stewart, "I feel like a boy again and am just crazy to get out." [2]

The hunt itself exceeded the hopes of the vice-president-elect. It began on January 11, 1901, at John Goff's ranch in the Danforth Hills north of Meeker and continued out of Keystone Ranch westward on Coyote Basin below an escarpment called Colorow Mountain. (Colorow was one of several Ute subchiefs who claimed to have fired the bullet that killed Major Thornburgh at Milk Creek.) During five weeks of "scampering" after Goff's hounds on the cold sage flats of Coyote Basin, the hunters bagged fourteen cougars. Roosevelt killed the largest himself—eight feet long to the tip of its tail and weighing a

1. Theodore Roosevelt letters to Philip B. Stewart, December 1900. Western Collection, Tutt Library, Colorado College, Colorado Springs, Colorado. Quoted by permission of John Wolcott Stewart.

2. Roosevelt letters. Colorado College.

record 227 pounds. He instructed Goff to ship the skin to the Smithsonian in Washington.

As a safety measure, Stewart had brought along on the hunt Dr. Gerald B. Webb, an English physician from Colorado Springs. Webb's services were not needed, though he stood ready to do repair work on one particular day. When the hunters spotted a cougar in a piñon tree, Stewart and Goff held Roosevelt's legs and lowered him headfirst from a bank above the tree to get him in a shooting position. Suddenly the animal lunged at him. Providentially, a hound intercepted the cougar, and it was the hound that Webb had to repair.

In the months that followed the hunt, Roosevelt discussed national conservation often with Gifford Pinchot, now chief of forestry in the Department of Agriculture, and fretted because tradition prevented vice-presidents from doing anything useful. During the summer he came to Colorado again and was pleased to find that public opinion was turning in favor of the forest reserves in Colorado because of a campaign conducted by an indefatigable writer of letters to the editor, Edgar T. Ensign, who was president of the Colorado Forest Association.

There was much talk in the state of new needs for irrigation water. The raising of sugar beets, Roosevelt learned, was spreading like wildfire. A sugar refinery costing half a million dollars had opened on the western slope in Grand Junction to serve growers using irrigation ditches along the Colorado River. Two other refineries were operating, at Rocky Ford and at Sugar City on the Arkansas. A shrewd German immigrant Charles Boettcher, who had made a fortune with a chain of Front Range hardware stores, had returned to Germany to retire. He became interested in the sugar-beet industry there and decided it would thrive in Colorado. Instead of retiring, he had come back to build half a dozen German-style refineries along the South Platte Valley. Many of his countrymen had followed him back to direct operation of the Boettcher refineries. Roosevelt observed that the growing of sugar beets was paying the farmers of Colorado so well that they could afford to enlarge their irrigation systems. Since cultivation of the beet required transient labor, thousands of workers and their families from Mexico moved to the South Platte and Arkansas River valleys to be absorbed later by the native Mexican-American ethnic group.

Roosevelt was intrigued by another pioneer development high in the San Juan Mountains near Telluride. This Ames plant, a hydroelectric turbine assembled in 1891 by Lucius Nunn and George Westinghouse, had proved that falling water could generate cheap power that could be delivered long distances by a new electrical system called alternating current. If power could be produced by falling water in the Ames turbine, why not use all those other billions of tons of water falling down from the Continental Divide to create energy for new industries? The thought gave Roosevelt a clear view of what a reclamation enthusiast from Nevada, Congressman Francis G. Newlands, was talking about when he argued that the forces of useful gravity belonged to the nation as a whole, and not just to the state where the gravity happened to be.

On August 9, 1901, the vice-president boarded, in Colorado Springs, the gold-painted club car of the new Short Line railroad to Cripple Creek, which had been built by Winfield Scott Stratton and others to break the ore-hauling monopoly of the Midland Terminal line, owned by Spencer Penrose and A. E. Carlton. It was a hair-raising trip of forty-two miles, winding around the south side of Pikes Peak on narrow shelves cut in the cliffs. (The roadbed is an automobile road today.) This time the miners of Victor greeted Roosevelt cordially. When one of them asked how he liked the Short Line trip, he replied, "Bully! This is the trip that bankrupts the English language!" [3]

And then, out of the blue, he found himself no longer the in-

3. Marshall Sprague, *Money Mountain* (Boston: Little, Brown and Co., 1953), p. 245.

effectual vice-president. On September 6, 1901, McKinley was shot in Buffalo, New York, by a Polish anarchist. He died of the wound eight days later.

Within days of his accession, the twenty-sixth and youngest president of the United States began making plans to implement his conviction that much of the mountain west should be held in trust by the government for the benefit of all the people. In April 1902, he withdrew by proclamation the huge San Isabel Timber Reserve in Colorado, which included most of the Sangre de Cristo Range above the San Luis Valley and the eastern slopes of the Saguache Range from Monarch Pass north to Tennessee Pass. Month by month thereafter he gobbled up more of the Colorado Rockies—the Gunnison Reserve, an enlarged Pikes Peak Reserve stretching from Cheyenne Mountain at Colorado Springs to the Continental Divide beyond Kenosha Pass, the Holy Cross Reserve above Colorado River, the Uncompahgre above Ouray, the Medicine Bow north of Denver. There were protests, but they were muted, as a result of widely circulated tales of frauds in which railroads, lumbermen, and ranchers were said to be looting the public domain with the connivance of underlings in the Department of the Interior.

And most Coloradans approved when Roosevelt yanked his reserves out of the tainted jurisdiction of the Interior Department and put them in Agriculture with a new blanket name, National Forests, in a new department—the U. S. Forest Service, headed by Gifford Pinchot. The personnel was increased from a handful to several hundred trained foresters. To educate them, Pinchot persuaded a number of universities to establish schools of forestry including one in Colorado, at Colorado College. Pinchot's foresters earned their keep by practices that revolutionized forest management in the United States—reseeding of trees, erosion control, rotation grazing, fire protection, wildlife study, and trail systems to encourage outdoor recreation. Sometimes his field employees headed off wars. In his book *Where the Old*

West Stayed Young John Rolfe Burroughs described how one forest supervisor, Harry Ratcliff, kept some peace between sheepmen and cattlemen in Routt National Forest by ruling that the sheep be confined to grasslands at altitudes higher than those preferred by cattle.[4]

In 1904, Colorado voters helped Roosevelt win the presidential election by giving him a huge majority. Thirty thousand people, the largest crowd in the state's history, gathered to hear him in Denver during his campaign tour. Everyone applauded when the news got out that he had showed up for a cowboy breakfast at the tailgate of a chuckwagon in Hugo clad in silk hat, frock coat, and winged collar. But the easy progress of his conservation program could not last. By the end of 1906, Roosevelt's national forests in the West had reached a total area of 107 million acres. Many Coloradans decided that he had to be stopped before the whole state ended up as a Roosevelt reserve.

And they thought that they had stopped him when Congress passed an act providing that no new reserves could be created by simple presidential proclamation after March 4, 1907. An act of Congress would be required from then on. Two days before the act became law, Roosevelt set aside twenty-one new national forests with an area of more than forty million acres. The additions raised the total in Colorado to eighteen forests totaling almost sixteen million acres—close to one quarter of the state's sixty-six million acres. As one bitter critic pointed out, Coloradans had worked hard to win that amount of land from the Utes in 1881. Now it was taken from them by a fast-talking outlander from faraway Oyster Bay, New York.

In this same period, another kind of reservation—to preserve antiquities—had its origins in Colorado. We have noted that F. V. Hayden's surveyors toured the mesas of southwestern Colorado in the 1870s and found superb cliff dwellings and ar-

4. John Rolfe Burroughs, *Where the Old West Stayed Young* (New York: William Morrow and Co., 1962), pp. 280–291.

tifacts left behind a thousand years and more ago by prehistoric Pueblo Indians. Soon souvenir hunters began swarming through the mesas carrying off ancient pottery, tools, cooking utensils, and even stones and bricks of the dwellings to sell to museums as far away as Sweden. Some promoters in Manitou Springs decided that it was more convenient to see these antiques at Pikes Peak than Mesa Verde, three hundred and fifty miles away. They spent a hundred thousand dollars blasting out a cave near Manitou and filling it with artifacts and cliff dwellings improvised from some forty carloads of stone, which they picked up in the Mesa Verde area. They opened their display to tourists under the same name that it has today, Manitou Springs Cliff Dwellings Museum.

To stop these depredations, a group of Colorado women organized the Cliff Dwellers Association to lobby in Washington for a national park at Mesa Verde. The women were inspired in their drive by many advances in the Colorado feminist movement, which had occurred during the 1890s, starting with the winning of the right to vote in 1893. That victory had made Colorado, as we have noted, the second state in the Union (after Wyoming) to grant that right. A smaller but still important advance happened that same year when a thirty-four-year-old professor of English from Wellesley College, Katherine Lee Bates, was assigned to the normally all-male faculty of Colorado College at Pikes Peak for the summer session. On an outing with the novelist Hamlin Garland and other teachers, Miss Bates rode in a wagon up the new carriage road to the top of Pikes Peak. She wrote of the trip later:

> Our sojourn on the peak remains in memory hardly more than one ecstatic gaze. It was then and there, as I was looking out over the sealike expanse of fertile country spreading away so far under these ample skies, that the opening lines of the hymn floated into my mind.[5]

5. Dorothy Burgess, *Dream and Deed* (Norman: University of Oklahoma Press, 1952), p. 102.

Miss Bates sold her hymn for a few dollars to *The Congrega-tionalist* magazine in 1895. Soon thereafter, when it was set to the music of Samuel Ward's "Materna," it became—and re-mains—the nation's favorite patriotic poem under the title "America the Beautiful."

Inspired by such samples of feminine achievement in Col-orado, the women of the Mesa Verde preservation lobby went to work with confidence. Some of them had the support of influ-ential husbands, Luna Thatcher, for example, was the wife of the Pueblo financial kingpin Mahlon D. Thatcher. Virginia Mc-Clurg of Colorado Springs, who headed the Cliff Dwellers As-sociation, was not shy about prodding Philip Stewart to get her demands through to his hunting friend President Roosevelt.

A major problem was that the best dwellings at Mesa Verde—Cliff Palace, Spruce Tree Lodge, Balcony House—were on Ute lands, the owners of which were willing to lease them if Mrs. McClurg could get a quorum of chiefs to agree on terms. "We donned bloomers and hiked our legs off chasing chiefs," Mrs. McClurg wrote later.

> They were out in the wilds most of the time foraging for the scanty subsistence denied them by the government. An Indian is an anomalous landlord. He comes up bright and smiling with every new moon to suggest an entire change in demands. He does not disdain to cement these treaties with Cyrano chains, Waterbury watches, watermelons, and striped candy.[6]

Mrs. McClurg did get her chiefs together at last and nego-tiated a ten-year lease with them, but the Department of the In-terior refused to approve it on technical grounds. Still, the Col-orado women persevered, pushing their cause through Congress after Congress. And on June 26, 1906, they won finally when President Roosevelt signed a bill passed by both houses creating Mesa Verde National Park, with provisions to protect the ruins

6. Edmund B. Rogers, "Notes on the Establishment of Mesa Verde National Park," *Colorado Magazine* 29:13–14 (January 1952).

on Ute lands within five miles of park boundaries. Seven years later Congress ratified a treaty with the Weminuche Utes, bringing the ruins on their land into the park and giving it the present area of 52,036 acres.

The Newlands Reclamation Act, which was designed to create vast areas of cropland out of worthless desert, was signed by Roosevelt on June 7, 1902. Its aims had been foreshadowed thirty years before when President Grant had proposed a federal canal running from Denver to the edge of the Kansas rain belt at the hundredth meridian to transform by irrigation the high, dry plains into gardens. It was known even then that controlled irrigation made lands more productive than uncontrolled rainfall. Though irrigation by local initiative had succeeded in some places like Greeley, private capital was not up to the financing of reservoirs and canals to bring water to all the arid regions that could benefit from it. The Homestead Act of 1862 and its later modifications to get the public domain into private ownership had failed, often because the size of the homestead could not be made to fit the variety of growing conditions west of the hundredth meridian. The Newlands Act was designed to eliminate this problem. Each farmer's homestead of from forty to one hundred and sixty acres would have the same potential as any other farmer's irrigated claim, regardless of location. The homesteads would make money and yet be small enough to bring enough farmers to an irrigated area to create a community. Though the homesteader would have to pay the government an annual fee of one dollar an acre for his water, it was presumed that he could afford the fee because of the high yields on his irrigated claim.

The new Reclamation Service planned its first venture in the Sterling area east of the mountains, but that was dropped when farmers on the western slope complained that they had more land needing irrigation and more water flowing by unused. An early and easy project of the Reclamation Service was the building of a dam and a high-line canal, which brought Grand (Col-

orado) River water to the western-slope fruit and sugar-beet
farms along a sixty-two-mile stretch from the village of Palisade
through Grand Junction to the Utah border. Another western-
slope project turned out to be far from easy. It involved the
diversion of water from Gunnison River through a tunnel to the
fertile but water-shy valley of the Uncompahgre River around
the towns of Montrose and Delta.

Just why Reclamation Service officials should have picked
one of the most difficult spots on earth for the east portal of
what would be at the time the longest irrigation tunnel in the
world—5.8 miles—remains a mystery. The starting point was in
the dankest and deepest part of the Black Canyon of the Gunnison, that narrow fifty-mile gorge with sheer granite walls rising as high as three thousand feet above the river. It was so
shaded down there that the resident rainbow trout acquired a
dismal, dark color. Its rushing waters and huge boulders were
not fully explored until 1882–1883, when Byron H. Bryant of
the Denver and Rio Grande Railroad led his engineers through
to the junction of the Gunnison and its north fork below Paonia.

Nobody else got through Black Canyon until 1901 when a
Montrose utilities man, William W. Torrence, and A. Lincoln
Fellows, a hydrographer for the U. S. Geographical Survey,
conquered the gorge by swimming and wading, and by tumbling
on rubber air mattresses over rapids too swift to be waded. The
nature writer Richard Beidleman has told how the two explorers
came one day to a place where the river vanished beneath a rock
slide. They shook hands in mock farewell and let the torrent
carry them on their mattresses wherever it was going. When
they emerged safely into daylight below the slide, they climbed
to a ledge and danced a jig.[7]

Many months were spent surveying for the irrigation tunnel to
connect the Gunnison with the watershed of the Uncompahgre.

7. Richard G. Beidleman, "The Gunnison River Diversion Project," *The Colorado Magazine* 36:187–201 (July 1959).

Blasting began in January 1905, and the bore was finished in July 1909. The workers had to endure ninety-degree heat, carbonic gas, and subsurface streams bursting through their drill holes. Nine men lost their lives. The tunnel was supposed to cost $1,500,000. The actual cost was $6,715,074. A year later, Gunnison water was reaching the irrigation ditches of the Uncompahgre. As a consequence, some 146,000 acres of reclaimed cropland valued at $30,000,000 was added to the resources of the people of Montrose and Delta counties.

The Uncompahgre Valley Project was the nation's first large-scale diversion of water for irrigation from the drainage system of one river to another. During the same period, the Denver banker David H. Moffat toiled to achieve a different kind of miracle—the building of a standard-gauge railroad over the highest part of the Continental Divide due west of Denver. Such a railroad was the old impossible dream of W. A. H. Loveland and John Evans to put Denver and Golden on a direct transcontinental route to San Francisco by way of Salt Lake City.

Moffat was in his sixties when he embarked on his great adventure, having concealed until then behind a screen of orthodox behavior the recklessness of his spirit. In the 1870s he had made money with Jerome Chaffee in the First National Bank of Denver and in the Caribou silver mine near Boulder. In the 1880s he had made more money with Chaffee and Horace Tabor in the Little Pittsburg at Leadville. In the 1890s he had struck it rich at Cripple Creek. When his railroad dream seized him in 1902, he was the richest and most powerful man in the Rockies.

The Denver and Rio Grande Railroad had been running to its West-Coast connections at Salt Lake City for many years by dipping from Denver south to Pueblo and then angling westward through the Royal Gorge of the Arkansas. Moffat's proposed route to Salt Lake City was nearly two hundred miles shorter—550 miles over Rollins Pass (altitude, 11,680 feet). The route would be shorter still when Rollins Pass was eliminated by a six-mile tunnel under James Peak, which Moffat expected to build as soon as his line began to collect revenue from the ranchers of Middle Park and the coal operators of the Yampa Valley.

Moffat was no amateur railroad man. He had served for a time as president of the Denver and Rio Grande, during which he spent a lot of D. and R. G. money investigating the James Peak tunnel matter. In 1894 he had won a race with the Colorado Midland people by getting his narrow-gauge Florence and Cripple Creek Railroad to the gold camp ahead of their line. He knew the risks that he was taking, even though he had a personal fortune of nine million dollars behind him—a huge sum in those days. He had seen how the high cost of mountain railroading had brought bankruptcy to the three little cliff-hanging lines that Otto Mears had built in the San Juans, and to the Colorado Midland out of Colorado Springs which had crossed Hagerman Pass above Leadville at first by a tunnel at 11,528 feet and then by a lower tunnel at 10,944 feet. Heavy snows had closed these lines for months at a stretch. He knew also that he would be opposed in a variety of ways by those greedy and unprincipled Eastern tycoons Edward H. Harriman of the Union Pacific and George Gould of the Missouri Pacific. But he had observed their skulduggery in Colorado for a decade, and he believed that he could match wits with them.

However, his first challenge came not from them but from the U. S. Reclamation Service, the officials of which were planning to use Gore Canyon as a site for a hydroelectric power and storage dam. This canyon was a deep trench through which the Grand (Colorado) River ran west of Kremmling. Moffat considered it to be the only practical way to get his road out of Middle Park and into the Yampa valley. His suits to win a right-of-way and to block the dam project dragged on and on while his crews were laying his tracks over Rollins Pass and across Middle Park. By 1905, his case seemed so hopeless that he sent his surveyors looking for another route. But suddenly word came that his application had been granted. The grantor was President Roosevelt, who told the press that the Moffat road would open northwest Colorado to settlement and improve communications between the western and eastern slopes, which gave it priority over the power project.

In his book *Rails That Climb* Edward T. Bollinger has described how Moffat's construction crews endured unbelievable hardships and tragedy in their efforts to build the line across the divide and on toward Craig. Meanwhile, Moffat sold his personal properties one by one to pay soaring construction costs— his gold and silver mines, his Denver Tramway stock, his major interest in the First National Bank. There were milestone dates to keep up his hopes—trains to the top of Rollins Pass on September 2, 1904, beyond Gore Canyon to McCoy on May 15, 1908, through the Oak Creek coalfields to Steamboat Springs on February 13, 1909. But Moffat's costs—ranging from $78,000 to $200,000 a mile—were many times higher than his original estimates. They brought him to the end of his millions in 1911, and to the end of his hopes and strength as well. As a last desperate measure, he swallowed his pride and went to New York to ask Harriman for help. Harriman was agreeable—in exchange for control of the railroad. Moffat refused, and died penniless in New York soon after, on May 20, 1911, at the age of seventy-one. His place as president of the Moffat Road was filled by John Evans's son William G., who rallied friends to save the line. With their support Evans was able to build on from Steamboat Springs forty-one miles farther to Craig by November 1913. Craig was where Moffat's dream ended.[8]

While Roosevelt's conservation policies were putting much of Colorado under federal control, another development, the deflation of mining, was bringing changes to the conduct of industry

8. Edward T. Bollinger, *Rails That Climb* (Santa Fe: Rydal Press, 1950), pp. 267–268.

in the state. The totally unexpected discovery of gold at Cripple Creek offset to a degree the decline of silver mining in 1893, but the Cripple Creek boom tapered off after 1900 when gold production reached a peak value of $18,200,000 from 475 shipping mines. By the end of World War I, production had declined to $5,867,511 from forty-one shipping mines.

A major effect of this deflation was the merging of companies in Colorado into large corporations to increase efficiency, to reduce competition, and to gain power by combination. The Swiss-born Jew Meyer Guggenheim and his son Simon, who got their start mining silver in Leadville, absorbed the state's leading smelters under the name of the American Smelting and Refining Company. Simon became a U. S. senator from Colorado in 1907. Charles Boettcher bunched his sugar refineries into the Great Western Sugar Company. John C. Osgood, who reorganized the Colorado Fuel and Iron Company at Pueblo out of the original Colorado Coal and Iron Company of General Palmer, was forced to turn over control of his firm to the Rockefeller interests.

Deflation and mergers had an effect on Colorado politics too. The mine owners used the power of their combinations to buy the election of James H. Peabody as Republican governor in 1902. Reaction set in two years later when the Democrat Alva Adams polled more votes than Peabody for the governorship. So much fraud was practiced in the contest that both Republicans and Democrats demanded a new election. In a weird attempt to save the honor of the state from the corruption of its parties, the general assembly named Peabody as governor, replacing Adams who had already held the office for two months. By agreement, Peabody resigned the same day in favor of the lieutenant governor, Jesse F. McDonald. Three governors in twenty-four hours!

It was inevitable that the mine workers of the state should band together to protect themselves against the combinations of the mine owners. They had at their disposal the most aggressive and successful union in the nation, the Western Federation of Miners, which was formed in Butte, Montana, in 1893, and which had won a great victory at Cripple Creek a year later when it forced the mine owners to meet its demands for an eight-hour day and a three-dollar-a-day wage. The WFM increased its power steadily, but its objectives shifted, meanwhile, from mere unionism to world revolution in an unofficial partnership with the International Workers of the World. In 1904 the WFM struck three gold reduction mills in Colorado City near Colorado Springs. The mill workers were joined seven months later by several hundred Cripple Creek miners—an early example of the sympathy strike.

James Peabody, the creature of the mine owners, was governor at the time. The state militia, which he sent to Cripple Creek, had orders to defend the mines, not the miners. The public generally took a neutral view of the conflict until June 6, 1904, when the WFM made a ghastly error. Two of its terrorists blew up a depot in the gold camp, covering part of Battle Mountain with the dismembered bodies of thirteen miners and wounding a dozen more. The union had supposed that the mine owners would be blamed for the blast, but the evidence showed clearly that the WFM was behind it. As public opinion turned against the union, the mine owners won the strike by the blatant suspension of all civil rights. The union was outlawed in Colorado. Seventy-three of its alleged ringleaders were loaded on flatcars by armed militiamen, hauled to the Kansas border, and dumped out on the prairie. That was the end of the Western Federation of Miners as a labor union in Colorado.

For nearly a decade thereafter, workers and owners lived in peace, until the United Mine Workers demanded to be recognized in the coal mines of the state. A showdown strike on the issue was called in September 1913 north of Trinidad at the Ludlow mine of the Colorado Fuel and Iron Company, which was still a Rockefeller subsidiary. The company reacted in the usual way. Strikebreakers were imported, and the governor was asked to send in militiamen to protect them.

The striking miners and their families withdrew to tent colonies near the mine. After a bitter winter, the climax came on April 20, 1914, when militiamen and strikers began shooting at one another. Five miners and one soldier died. The militia set fire to the tents which brought death by burning or suffocation to two women and eleven children. President Woodrow Wilson sent the regular army to restore order and arrange housing for the burned-out families. Peace talks dragged on until December 1914, when the United Mine Workers agreed to withdraw from Colorado, and state legislature passed measures to improve conditions in the mines.

John D. Rockefeller, Jr., had never seen any of his Colorado mines and knew nothing about their operation. Appalled by the tragedy at Ludlow, he went there in September 1915, and spent a fortnight discussing grievances with the miners. The result was "the Rockefeller Plan," an extensive program for higher wages, shorter hours, freedom to deal or not to deal at company stores, and no discrimination against workers who joined a union. The coal miners of the state approved the plan overwhelmingly, and it was adopted later by many American companies until its inherent paternalism was outdated by the Wagner Act of 1935.

A good many Coloradans actually had no particular interest in these issues that were troubling the state up to the beginning of World War I. They were absorbed in the growth of an industry based on nothing more tangible than the longing people had to enjoy themselves.

8

Tourists and the Twenties

*F*ROM the days of the Dominguez-Escalante expedition and of Zebulon Pike, people had talked about the charms of these highest Rocky Mountains. Artists with the early explorers—Titian Peale with the Long expedition, Richard Kern with Frémont and Gunnison—depicted them in dramatic sketches. In 1867 Bayard Taylor, the celebrated poet and world traveler, published an enormously popular book *Colorado: A Summer Trip,*[1] which attracted thousands to the mining regions, not to get rich but just to look around.

Four years later, General William J. Palmer laid out and widely publicized his dream town at the foot of Pikes Peak, a town that had nothing to do with mining or ranching or any other respectable industry. Colorado Springs was the first genuine resort west of Chicago, and Palmer designed its wide streets lined with shade trees to test an odd theory of his—that aesthetics and good taste in a real estate development would pay off commercially. Though it had no springs, Palmer named it Colorado Springs because most of the fashionable resorts back East had the word *springs* attached to their names.

1. Bayard Taylor, *Colorado: A Summer Trip* (New York: G. P. Putnam and Son, 1867).

The general built it primarily as a place of residence for people of means who liked scenery, pleasant weather, and outdoor sports, or who thought that the climate would cure their consumption or asthma. Rowdies were not welcome. Refinement was the watchword. Palmer permitted no houses of prostitution or dance halls within the city limits, and he banned saloons, though he had no objection to gentlemanly drinking. Many of those who settled there were Britishers who drank tea, dressed for dinner, and sang "God Save the Queen" on Victoria's birthday. To accommodate the transient tourist and health seeker, Palmer and his partner, William A. Bell, platted Manitou five miles away and installed there a talented English man of medicine Dr. Samuel E. Solly, whose ecstatic booklet on Manitou explained why its nauseous springs would positively cure anything, be it water brash or flatulence or catarrh of the genitourinary passages.

At this time Colorado Springs benefited from the alluring magazine articles about the Pikes Peak region by one of the nation's best-known literary figures, Helen Hunt, who went to Manitou in 1873 to see what Dr. Solly's miracle waters would do for her catarrh, and stayed on in Colorado Springs as the wife of a Denver and Rio Grande official, William S. Jackson. In that same year, an English writer Isabella Lucy Bird— "liberated woman" would describe her more accurately— bought a pony named Birdie in Longmont, donned a huge hat and Turkish trousers over her bloomers, and rode astride Birdie to an incipient dude ranch in an obscure upland intervale called Estes Park.

She boarded at the ranch for some months, with time out for a ride of five hundred miles alone on Birdie south to Colorado Springs, west to what is now Lake George, across the north end of South Park, and back over Kenosha Pass to Estes Park. A second interval was spent consorting with a handsome Irish ne'er-do-well known only as Rocky Mountain Jim. She spent two days and two nights climbing Longs Peak with Jim. (The spot that he picked for her nighttime "bower of evergreens" is still called Jim's Grove.) Then she wrote all about it in a book called *A Lady's Life in the Rocky Mountains*.[2] This "scandalous" true confession, a best seller to this day, brought instant notoriety to Estes Park and was one reason why Windham Thomas Wyndham-Quinn, the fourth Earl of Dunraven and Montearl in the Peerage of Ireland, hurried to Estes during the next summer to set up a hunting lodge, game preserve, and hotel. The spot for the hotel facing Longs Peak was chosen by Albert Bierstadt, whose painting of the peak adorns the reading room of the Western Collection in the Denver Public Library. Though none of Lord Dunraven's projects worked out very well, his pioneering marked the beginning of Estes Park as a resort.

Colorado Springs and Estes Park were designed for those with time on their hands. But most visitors to Colorado through the 1870s and for three decades thereafter were short-termers in search of excitement. The tourism which they created was a by-product of the remarkable system of narrow-gauge and standard-gauge railroads which had been built for the mining industry. Every paying mine at no matter what dizzy height along the spine of the Continental Divide came to be reached by one of the railroads—the narrow-gauge D. and R. G., perhaps on a spur to Creede, or the standard-gauge Colorado Midland to Basalt and Aspen, or the Denver and South Park to Breckenridge, or the Colorado Central to the old Gilpin County diggings, or Otto Mears's little cliff crawlers serving Gladstone and Telluride.

This accessibility into the stratosphere was unparalleled not only in the West but in the world. The railroad companies wasted no time providing luxury equipment to entice tourists to their trains. Blushing newlyweds boarded Pullman palace

2. Isabella Bird, *A Lady's Life in the Rocky Mountains* (London: John Murray, 1879).

sleepers and pinned their marriage licenses outside their berths before retiring. The menus of diners offered quail and antelope and champagne. From the verandas of rococo observation cars ladies and gentlemen gasped in terror as the train rattled over spindly trestles on the Cripple Creek run or groaned up Marshall Pass en route to Gunnison, or up Hagerman Pass short of Aspen, or over Lizard Head above Rico. The Georgetown Loop to Silver Plume was recommended highly for scaring people to death and so was the circling Cumbres Pass trip from Alamosa to Durango, during which engine and caboose passed one another three times while gaining altitude for the crossing.

The luxury rail traffic brought luxury hotels to replace the crude log inns of the mining towns soon after the tracks arrived. In *No More Than Five in a Bed* Sandra Dallas has described these Victorian hostelries, many of which thrive today. At Central City Henry Teller's Teller House (1872) featured in its bar life-sized statues of Leda and Venus, Aphrodite and Juno, and other plump charmers of the long ago appropriately unclad to support the claims of the management that the bar was "well supplied with things to cheer and inebriate." [3] At Georgetown the reticent Frenchman Louis Dupuy opened his elegant Hotel de Paris in 1875 and reigned for twenty years as the greatest chef in the Rockies.

In Durango young Henry Strater opened the Hotel Strater (1882) with wood-burning stoves in every room and an adjoining Pisa-like column of privies three stories high. The La Veta Hotel (1884) in Gunnison was so magnificent that it failed of its own extravagance, even though trains of the D. and R. G. stopped a few feet from the lobby and its owner offered free board and room to guests for any day that the sun failed to shine. The railroads were late building to Aspen, which explains why the handsome Hotel Jerome, a Victorian masterpiece, was

3. Sandra Dallas, *No More than Five in a Bed* (Norman: University of Oklahoma Press, 1967), p. 55.

not opened until 1889. Its proprietor, Jerome Wheeler, called the Jerome "the handsomest hotel on the Western Slope" and he equipped it with such modern devices as electric lights and an elevator, which the passenger operated by pulling on ropes.[4] The rope elevator has been replaced, but in other Victorian respects the Hotel Jerome of 1976 is much the same as it was in the nineties.

Surveyors for the ubiquitous railroads became adept at finding medicinal hot springs along their rights-of-way, which gave the lines more plush hotels to serve, and more bathhouses where the ailing could boil the poisons from their systems. A pioneer health hotel was the Cliff House (1874) at Manitou Springs. Another was the Beebee House in Idaho Springs, which did poorly until 1881, when it was found that the springs of Soda Creek contained quantities of the miracle mineral radium. The Beebee house gave way to the huge Radium Hot Springs Hotel, built right over the magic waters to which, the proprietors declared, "the stretcher is carried in only one direction." [5] Trimble Hot Springs and Hotel, a favorite with miners suffering from lead poisoning, opened near Durango in 1882 with a D. and R. G. depot at one end of the croquet court. The Antero Hotel and Mount Princeton Hot Springs prospered not far up Chalk Creek on the line of the Denver and South Park running to Gunnison.

Of all these health spas, the most spectacular was the Hotel Colorado at Glenwood Springs. It was built in 1893 at a cost of $850,000 by a New York mining engineer Walter B. Devereux and his sons Horace and James. It had two hundred bedrooms, nearly a hundred baths, a dining room as big as a basketball court, and a ballroom seventy-two feet long and twenty-four feet wide. A $100,000 stone bridge led from the hotel to the great mineral pool, the waters of which stood at ninety-two

4. Dallas, *Five in a Bed*, p. 73.
5. Dallas, *Five in a Bed*, p. 182.

degrees Fahrenheit the year round. The Devereux men were famed polo players, and their hotel manager Harvey Lyle was a national star. From the hotel veranda, visitors could watch games on the hotel's polo field between the Glenwood team and a team from Denver or Colorado Springs. The Hotel Colorado catered strictly to the famous or the very rich or both. Theodore Roosevelt might be registered there, or P. D. Armour or Diamond Jim Brady or Buffalo Bill. To stress its high standing with nabobs, the hotel was equipped with a railroad siding large enough to hold sixteen private cars. One of the spaces was reserved for whatever president of the United States might unexpectedly drop in for a warm swim.

The evolution of this minor tourism by rail into a major Colorado industry was foreshadowed in 1900 when a pioneer automobile manufacturer John Brisben Walker drove his Locomobile up the Pikes Peak carriage road as far as Glen Cove with the help of a brace of strong mules. Two years later, a Denver auto sales agent, W. B. Felker, made it to the top unaided in his Locomobile. The engine of Felker's car was a steam model, the patents of which Walker had bought experimentally in 1899 and sold back to its inventors, twin brothers named Freelan and Francis Stanley.

These ingenious twins, born in Maine in 1849, were manufacturing dry plates for photography near Boston in 1900, a process they would sell soon to the Eastman Kodak Company for a million dollars. Their next project was building two-cylinder, thirty-horse-power, kerosene-fueled Stanley Steamer cars. When Freelan Stanley's friend Walker, the Locomobile man, told him of the beauties of Colorado and what automobiles could do to bring those beauties to the masses, Freelan freighted a Stanley Steamer to Denver in June 1903 and drove it up St. Vrain Canyon by way of Longmont to Estes Park to see if Walker was telling the truth. He made the forty-mile trip on the rough St. Vrain stage road in less than two hours, which was ten times faster than the record time for the trip by stage.

In 1903 Freelan Stanley was evaporating rapidly from the ravages of tuberculosis. (He weighed only a hundred pounds.) But the majestic scenery of Longs Peak and the Continental Divide lifted his spirits. The climate of Estes—crisp, cool nights and sunny days splashed with brief afternoon showers, braced him wonderfully. He gained weight and strength and began taking long walks with a slender, red-haired, voluble young innkeeper named Enos Mills, whose romantic notions about the future of Estes Park impressed Stanley deeply. Mills was a Lincolnesque character who had packed his thirty-three years with an incredible amount of manual work, self-education, and adventure. He was born in 1870 on a Kansas farm and had left the cornfields to stake a homestead, at the age of sixteen, directly under Longs Peak. (He got his patent when he became of age and later his Longs Peak Inn adjoined the homestead.) For a dozen winters he had worked in the copper mines of Montana, and, in summer, guided parties to the top of Longs Peak, or anywhere else that visitors wanted to go in that welter of mountains, glaciers, timberline lakes, and forested canyons.

Mills's manner of living in those years was so spartan that a few dollars of saved wages were all he had needed to finance months of travel—to Alaska and Mexico and Yellowstone Park, to the High Sierras of California and the Swiss Alps. All the while he had read incessantly to teach himself to become what he actually was when Stanley met him in 1903—the first professional environmentalist in the Rockies. His inn turned out to be more of a workshop for students of wildlife than a business. In choosing this career, Mills had been encouraged and inspired by a much older man, the great conservationist John Muir, whose activities in California had led to the creation of Yosemite and Sequoia national parks.

Mills passed along to Stanley his idea about how tourists

ought to enjoy themselves in Colorado—not by taking the baths and riding scary trains, but by camping out, by hiking the mountain trails, by listening to the music of creeks and forest breezes, by studying the birds, wildflowers, trees, and animals. A knowledge of nature, Mills told Stanley, was the basis of wisdom, since everything man knew about beauty and truth came from his observation of natural forms, animate and inanimate.

Freelan Stanley found it easy to combine Mills's love of nature with the interests of the Stanley Motor Carriage Company. He saw that Estes Park had developed very slowly because of its isolation. What it needed was more Stanley Steamers to bring more nature lovers to Longs Peak quickly and easily from Lyons and Loveland. And the park needed a modern hotel to supplement the limited space in the handful of old-time lodges like Stead's, the Elkhorn, and Abner Sprague's. As a first step he bought Lord Dunraven's large holdings of land. Next, in 1907, he started a dozen Stanley Steamer Mountain Wagons shuttling to Estes from the plains towns on roads which he improved at his own expense. Two years later he designed and built, at a cost of half a million dollars, the Stanley Hotel, a sedate white clapboard echo of those White Mountain inns that he had known in New England. When tourists filled the Stanley to the rafters, he built a large addition in 1910—Stanley Manor.

Stanley's enterprise stimulated the growth of Estes Park enormously. In ten years after 1903, the number of summer visitors increased from a few hundred to fifty thousand. Many of these visitors became addicted to Enos Mills's rules for enjoying the outdoors. Meanwhile, Mills himself had achieved the stature of a national celebrity as a highly paid writer of books and articles on nature. He had no time for the outdoors now, being busy with a project that John Muir had suggested to him—to remove the national-forest part of Estes, which was most of it, from the jurisdiction of the Department of Agriculture and make it a national park under the Department of the Interior.

Mills found himself with an ugly and exhausting fight on his hands. The idealistic preservationist Gifford Pinchot had been dismissed as Forest Service chief in 1910. The new Forest Service was directed by men interested mainly in making money out of the forest reserves by the unrestricted sale of timber and grazing permits. These officials denied Mills's claim that such commercial activity would do great harm to the natural environment of Estes, and they did not want to lose the region to Agriculture's bitter rival, the Department of the Interior. They organized battalions of lumbermen and cattlemen to oppose Mills—a case of well-heeled Goliaths challenging one unsupported David.

But Mills had a compelling idea, and he found an admiring audience of millions as he lectured throughout the nation on the theme of "Room, glorious room, in which to find ourselves." And, in the end, he won his point, which was, in effect, that the interest of countless Americans in meeting a fat marmot on the Longs Peak trail was more important than the economic interests of a few. On January 26, 1915, President Wilson signed a bill creating the 400-square-mile Rocky Mountain National Park. Sixty years later, two million people were flocking to Longs Peak annually looking for marmots or whatever else Mills had made it possible for them to discover.

One man who watched the success of Stanley's hotel and his steamers with more than casual interest was Spencer Penrose of Colorado Springs. Penrose, a big, handsome Harvard graduate in his early fifties, had come to Pikes Peak from Philadelphia in 1892 and had made a vast amount of money, first at Cripple Creek and then by promoting a very profitable copper mine in Utah. He was the kind of man who ought to be rich, for he enjoyed the good things that money could buy—good food, good clothes, good whiskey—with the same zest that Enos Mills enjoyed spotting a pileolated warbler.

Penrose admired what Stanley's hotel and his steamer had done at Estes Park, and he decided to do some promoting of his own at Pikes Peak. As early as 1902, when a Springs friend of his, W. W. Price, drove his buggy-shaped Winton to Glenwood Springs over Tennessee Pass, Penrose had believed that the automobile would revolutionize life in the United States, and particulary in Colorado, beribboned as it was with mining roads. To counter the mining slump, he had backed the formation of the Colorado Good Roads Association in 1905, the Rocky Mountain Highway Association in 1908, and the State Highway Commission a year later, which became the State Highway Department. To show his own faith in cars, he tried a new kind every year, and then settled on four of them—all Loziers—for his personal use, at a cost of $5,000 each.

In 1913 he rejoiced when the Colorado highway department co-operated with the Forest Service to build the first auto road in the Rockies to cross the Continental Divide, the forty-two-mile Wolf Creek Pass highway, which is still one of the loveliest drives in the state. It replaced the often impassable Ellwood Pass wagon road between San Luis Valley and the San Juan mining region. But Penrose felt that the triumph at Wolf Creek was not publicized enough. To show more effectively the merits of motor cars in mountain travel, he transformed the old carriage road to the top of Pikes Peak (14,110 feet) into the highest auto road on earth—a vertical climb of 6,746 feet in seventeen miles. He expected it to cost $25,000, but he had spent a quarter of a million dollars before it was finished in October 1915. The following August he organized the first Pikes Peak Hill Climb auto race with the celebrated Berner Eli (Barney) Oldfield among his twenty racers. Rea Lentz won the race in a tiny eight-cylinder Romano—twenty minutes and fifty-five seconds on the twelve-mile run to the summit. Oldfield could do no better than to place twelfth in his French Delage.

The race was reported around the world, and its success as a Pikes Peak tourist attraction encouraged Penrose to embark on his next promotion—a resort hotel, but not in the prim and proper style of the Hotel Stanley at Estes, patronized by earnest nature lovers. Penrose had another kind of patronage in mind—

those rich Texans and Oklahomans and Kansans who vacationed abroad normally but could not do so now that a war was tearing Europe apart. To lure these frustrated hedonists to Pikes Peak, he planned a two-million-dollar establishment combining the most elegant features of the hotels that he himself had visited in Monte Carlo and Baden Baden, Cairo and Biarritz and Peking, with emphasis on all the expensive sports, plus a small zoo for the children. To design his hotel, Penrose chose the firm of Warren and Wetmore, who had shown talent for grandeur by building the Grand Central Station in New York. He called it The Broadmoor, and he placed it under Cheyenne Mountain on the site of the Count Pourtales Casino that had failed in the 1890s.

For elegance and variety, the Broadmoor outshone even the Hotel Colorado in Glenwood Springs, and the fading Antlers that General Palmer had built in downtown Colorado Springs. Penrose opened the Broadmoor on June 29, 1918, with a thoroughly European banquet prepared by an Italian chef, featuring a German band, sherry from Spain, and a French menu including *veloute de volaille* and braised sweetbreads *aux perles de Perigord*.

It was characteristic of Penrose that no little thing like a world war was going to delay his hotel construction plans. The first units of the American Expeditionary Force had arrived in France in 1917 to join the Allies in their struggle with Germany. It was a popular war in Colorado despite the misgivings of many German-born residents. People thought of Kaiser Wilhelm as the overdressed tyrant in the spiked hat who meant to make a Prussian colony out of their spacious state and substitute slavery for the freedom of their upland democracy. Some forty-three thousand Coloradans served in the army and navy. Those who stayed at home obeyed the pleas of President Wilson that they buy liberty bonds, wrap bandages, plant war gardens, and eat less meat.

A thousand Coloradans lost their lives in the sodden trenches of France before peace came with the armistice of November 11, 1918. The war brought some compensations. The dry-land farmers around Holyoke, Akron, Yuma, and Cheyenne Wells who had survived the drouths and depression of the 1890s made large profits on $2-a-bushel wheat. They bought Model-T Fords and improved their homes with modern plumbing and with windbreaks of locust and Russian olive trees. They bought windmills and steam tractors and multiple plows with which to carve up the grasslands to grow more wheat. The sugar-beet farmers prospered too, receiving twice the usual contract price for their beets from the refineries on the South Platte and Arkansas rivers. The beet growers had strong financial support from men like Charles Boettcher of Denver and George W. Swink of Rocky Ford, who had pioneered both beets and irrigation in the Arkansas Valley. Some of the transient labor for harvesting beets was supplied by revolutionists coming up the ancient Spanish trails from Mexico to earn money, which they would contribute to overthrow the Carranza government.

On the western slope the war caused a boomlet in a rare metal vanadium for hardening steel. It was a by-product of the uranium ore used by Marie Curie in 1898 when she discovered in it the radioactive element radium. Vanadium was mined in the hauntingly beautiful canyons of the Dolores and St. Miguel rivers that Dominguez and Escalante had explored during their rambling trek to Utah in 1776. Another steel-hardening metal called molybdenum was taken from Bartlett Mountain near the top of Fremont Pass (11,318 feet above sea level) on the Continental Divide north of Leadville. Molybdenum had a high melting point, but nobody knew much more about it in 1918, and it wasn't expected to come to anything.

Three years of hard times throughout the nation followed the ephemeral prosperity of the war period, though the hardship in Colorado was less severe than in most states. The fall in price of farm products was offset somewhat by co-operative marketing and improved methods of high-altitude agriculture. The new federal land banks offered low interest rates on loans in a program to reduce foreclosures on farms hit by the collapse of land values.

One post-war incident had no economic import, but it was applauded on both sides of the Continental Divide and tended to improve the abrasive relations that existed between east and west slopes. Until 1921, "Colorado River" signified the stream discovered by Coronado's men in 1540. It flowed to the Gulf of California from the mouth of present Green River in Utah. The other stream at the Green River confluence had been labeled "Grand River" in Hayden's atlas, which showed it crossing western Colorado from its sources in the future Rocky Mountain National Park. After Colorado won statehood, its citizens grew increasingly annoyed that no part of Colorado River was in Colorado. To meet their complaint, the Colorado legislature picked a day in 1921 when the Utah legislature was not in session to change "Grand River" to "Colorado River," forestalling a Utah plan to extend the name "Colorado River" to include the full length of Green River. Congress approved the Colorado action before the Utahans had time to organize a protest.

That same year of 1921 marked the start of one of the most serious aberrations in the state's history—the rise of the Ku Klux Klan under the Grand Dragonship of a strange Denver physician Dr. John Galen Locke. Many residents of Colorado, like Americans elsewhere, found themselves full of fears after World War I—fears of hard times, of the communism of Karl Marx, of Eugene Debs and his American socialism, of the Industrial Workers of the World and their violence, of spies in the land working for foreign governments. To these fearful people, especially in the Front Range cities, Locke's program of "One Hundred Percent Americanism" had great appeal. They found joy in Klan activities, dressing in sheets, burning crosses on Table Mountain near Golden and atop Pikes Peak, and boycott-

ing the businesses of their opponents. They persecuted Catholics
and Negroes and, especially, successful Jews such as Jesse
Shwayder, the son of a Polish immigrant who had created the
huge luggage firm, Samsonite Corporation. The Klansmen took
advantage of the unemployment to attack recent immigrants to
Colorado from Greece and Hungary who had jobs in the Denver
smelters around the Globeville section and at the C. F. & I.
steel works of South Pueblo—jobs which the Klan said should
be held by "real" Americans. The Klansmen advised Denverites to cease patronizing restaurants bearing "foreign"
names like Pagliacci or Benito or Ciancio or Wong or Torino.
By 1924 the Klan membership was large enough to elect the
state's governor, a senator, the mayor and chief of police of
Denver, and a majority in the general assembly. But within
months most of these Klansmen turned out to be inept public officials. And when Locke resigned in June of 1925 as Grand
Dragon after being jailed for contempt of court in an income-tax
matter, the power of the Klan ended abruptly and completely.

The rest of the decade passed pleasantly enough. As Stanley
and Penrose had hoped, cars replaced horses rapidly. The state
highway department was chronically short of funds, but some
progress was made in improving roads. By 1924 motorists in
summer were whisking over Berthoud Pass on a new road sixteen feet wide en route to Salt Lake City. Other drivers made it
from Ouray to Durango over what were called "the double hair-
pin loops" of the Million-Dollar Highway—so named because
its gravel was alleged to contain gold. Drivers with steady
nerves could manage a run over Kenosha Pass into South Park,
over Poncha Pass into San Luis Valley, and over what is known
today as Old Monarch Pass from Salida to Gunnison. (The
present Monarch Pass highway was opened in 1939.) In the fall
of 1928, the highway department assembled some homemade
snowplows at Leadville and achieved a miracle by keeping Tennessee Pass open all winter. Up to then, motorists wishing to

take their cars from Denver to the western slope had to freight them by rail across the Continental Divide.

Prohibition in the twenties was more of a nuisance than a problem in Colorado, which went dry in 1916, three years before passage of the national Volstead Act. Thomas Hornsby Ferril, the eminent Denver poet and essayist, has written nostalgically of the cheerful Italian speakeasies in north Denver where plenty of red wine went along with the spaghetti dinners.[6] Guests in Denver arriving at private cocktail parties often found the host at his bathtub making gin for the occasion. Ferril has described also the huge tonnages of sugar from the South Platte refineries that were shipped to Leadville, where many distilleries hidden in the hills transformed the product into illicit "Leadville moon." This fine sugar whiskey was supplied in five-gallon tins (price, $10) to customers all over the state by bootleggers driving Ford and Chevrolet sedans equipped with special springs to handle heavy liquid loads. Some bootleggers sold "Casper moon" from Wyoming and some specialized in "Red Lodge moon" from Montana, a liquor of such excellence that companies in Canada were said to bottle it for export to the United States as bonded whiskey.

No event of the twenties boosted the state's morale quite as much as what might be called Act Two in the three-act play based on David Moffat's railroad which we left stalled at Craig in 1913 under the presidency of William Gray Evans, son of the late ex-governor John Evans. As World War I ended, William Evans was seized by a passion—to realize Moffat's dream of a 6.2 mile tunnel under James Peak and to continue building the railroad from Craig to Salt Lake City. The tunnel would pierce James Peak at a point 2,400 feet below Rollins Pass, reduce the distance across the divide by twenty-three miles, and eliminate

6. Thomas Hornsby Ferril and Helen Ferril, *The Rocky Mountain Herald Reader* (New York: William Morrow and Co., 1966).

the grades, curves, and blizzards of the pass. And it would permit the line to achieve Moffat's second goal of bringing growth to the ranches of Middle Park and the coalfields and oil-shale deposits of northwestern Colorado. The pioneer bore of the tunnel would serve to test an old idea—the transfer of water from streams on the western slope to Denver's east-slope reservoirs.

For a state of moderate wealth and less than a million people, the Moffat Tunnel was a horrendous undertaking. At the time, only four tunnels of greater length existed on earth, all in heavily populated areas in or near the Swiss Alps, and at much lower altitudes—the twelve-mile Simplon, the nine-mile St. Gotthard, the nine-mile Lotschberg, and the eight-mile Mount Cenis. Robert G. Athearn has told the story well in his history of the Denver and Rio Grande *Rebel of the Rockies*—how William Evans fought to overcome the general skepticism about the project from 1913 on. Voters and state legislators turned down again and again the bond issues that he proposed to raise funds for the tunnel. Officials of the Missouri Pacific and Western Pacific blocked his plans in Congress and Wall Street. Their railroads connected with the Denver and Rio Grande, and they were about to buy the latter road. They wanted no competing shorter line across the state.

Evans got no help from the leaders of Pueblo and Southern Colorado who were perennially opposed to anything that would benefit Denver and the northern tier of counties. They refused to be seduced when he promised them tunnels of their own at Monarch Pass and at Cumbres Pass. And, in late May of 1921, he was forced to conclude that his cause was lost when the Moffat Road found itself close to bankruptcy after the line had run deficits of $100,000 a month for a year and more in the vain hope that the postwar slump would soon be over.

And then a bad kind of good fortune came to Evans's rescue. It began to rain hard in Pueblo on June 1, 1921. The Arkansas River rose slowly as the downpour continued into June 3, and residents were warned to move to higher ground. Some did move. "Others," Robert Athearn wrote,

> were morbidly curious. They jostled each other along the levees, anxious to see the display. At half-past eight that night, the torrent swept aside a breakwater west of the city, and a wall of water cascaded through its streets, carrying a mass of debris with it. The lights went out. Panic-stricken drivers gunned their engines, leaned on their horns, and joined the caravan of mad flight to higher ground. Minutes later a mile-wide swath of downtown Pueblo was submerged under twelve feet of water.[7]

A hundred residents of Pueblo and migrant workers living in tents along the Arkansas drowned that night in the worst flood in Colorado history. Damages to homes and office buildings exceeded sixteen million dollars. After the cleanup of dead horses, smashed autos and railroad cars and rubble, groups of Puebloans formed to demand flood-control districts. The result some months later—a double bill for flood control and a tunnel bond issue—was a surprise to many people but not to William Evans, who had been pulling wires at the statehouse to produce measures that would give Pueblo its flood control if the city supported his bond issue for the Moffat Tunnel.

The double bill passed, the tunnel was built, and five years later, on February 26, 1928, a twenty-car passenger train roared through this unique property of the State of Colorado, the initial cost of which was $15,470,000. William Evans was not among the officials on that first train. Like David Moffat before him, he had worn himself out on Denver's seventy-year-old dream of conquering the great Rockies barrier to the West and had died in 1924 at the age of sixty-eight. Gerald Hughes, a son of Senator Charles J. Hughes, assumed the Evans role in the Moffat Road drama, which floundered through a dull Act Three of intermina-

7. Robert G. Athearn, *Rebel of the Rockies* (New Haven: Yale University Press, 1962), pp. 269–270.

ble maneuverings by the state tunnel authority, the Denver and
Rio Grande, half a dozen transcontinental railroads, and the
U. S. government.

The climax came in 1934 when Denver found itself on a
direct line at last to Salt Lake City and San Francisco, but not
on the tracks of the Moffat Road, which was fated to remain
forever stalled at Craig. The Denver and Rio Grande had won
the tunnel route by buying the Moffat Road and building a
forty-mile link between the D. and R. G. station at Dotsero,
near the head of Glenwood Canyon and a point on the Moffat
called Orestod, where that line emerged from Gore Canyon, of
the Colorado. "Dotsero" was alleged to be the name of a beautiful Ute Indian maid who loved railroads. "Orestod" became a
name when some doodler thought of spelling Dotsero back-
wards.

On the whole, the twenties were good years for Coloradans,
in spite of their disenchantment with the aftermath of the war.
The motor car brought them not only the economic benefits of
an expanding tourism but a greatly enlarged playground for their
own enjoyment. Airplanes were hauling mail and passengers
before the decade ended. A boom in oil began in 1925. Three
years later, the United Mine Workers union, which had with-
drawn from the state in 1914 after the Ludlow tragedy, returned
to sign a contract with the Rocky Mountain Fuel Company
owned by the militant and progressive feminist Josephine
Roche—a contract "to establish industrial justice, substitute
reason for violence . . . and a union of effort for the chaos of
present economic warfare." [8] This historic document paved the
way for a new era in the nation's labor relations.

While old-timers mourned the death of gold-mining and
silver-mining, a talented writer and artist Muriel Sibell Wolle

8. *Colorado: A Guide to the Highest State* (New York: Hastings House, 1941, 1970),
p. 58.

was scrambling around the hills discovering and sketching what remained of several hundred ghost towns of the argonauts so that they would never be forgotten. The result of her searches was a huge and wonderful book called *Stampede to Timberline*, which endures as a Colorado classic.[9]

Of course a small cloud appeared with the stock-market crash of October 29, 1929. But Wall Street was far, far away, and Coloradans did not believe that the small cloud would darken the blue skies of their sunny empire.

9. Muriel Sibell Wolle, *Stampede to Timberline* (Boulder: University of Colorado Press, 1949).

9

Breadlines and
the Big T

$\mathcal{C}$OLORADANS read the headlines in their newspapers—

STOCK EXCHANGE HAS WILDEST DAY IN HISTORY

—and the soothing remarks of President Hoover about the crash, and passed on to stories that intrigued them more, such as the trial of the Fleagle gang of Kansas bank robbers who had murdered four prominent citizens of Lamar. A majority of citizens remained calm for months as the financial crisis deepened nationally and the paper value of American industry was cut in half. The effects of the depression spread to Colorado slowly. Automobile tourism held up through 1930 because of low prices for gasoline and for lodging in the new cottage camps. Thousands from out of state came to see the lower stretches of the Trail Ridge Road which was being built from Estes Park across the Continental Divide to Grand Lake, reaching 12,183 feet above sea level at its highest point near Milner Pass. And there was a small boom in rich Indian tourists from Oklahoma riding in their new Cadillacs and Pierce Arrows driven by black chauffeurs.

This initial apathy was almost a neurosis—a disinclination of the average Coloradan to face up to any problems just then. He was tired of problems, having endured mining deflation for forty years to say nothing of confusing politics—populism, the silver issue, Roosevelt's theft of his forests, Bull Moose progressivism, Wilsonian democracy, the "normalcy" of Harding and Coolidge, and the nightmare regime of Grand Dragon Locke. His disenchantment with these matters made him anxious to have a little peace under the leadership of William H. "Billy" Adams, who was elected governor in 1927.

Billy Adams—the boyish nickname used by everybody was significant—was sixty-six years old when he became governor. He had arrived at that age as trim and spry as any cowboy of half his years, and that was what he was—a cheerful, outgoing, bowlegged cowboy, trained to keep the fences tight and not wear out the horses. He was also an able rancher with a large cattle spread in San Luis Valley, where he had lived since 1878. His constituents loved him because he believed in what they believed in—the old pioneer spirit, self-reliance, hard work, getting the job done. He was nominally a Democrat like his much older brother Alva, three times a governor of Colorado, but his views were those of a conservative Republican, and he applied them to the conduct of his office when the depression began. His program called for rigid economy, balancing the state budget, resisting federal encroachment on Colorado's affairs, and trusting the common sense of his people to cope with the depression through private charities and relief measures at the county level. But Adams did not choose to run for a third term in 1932. He retired to his ranch and helped his protegé Edwin Carl Johnson, aged forty-eight, win the governorship in the election that fall.

"Big Ed" Johnson, born a Kansan of Swedish Lutheran parentage, had settled in northwest Colorado in 1909 and had worked as homesteader, railroad hand, telegrapher, and schoolteacher before becoming manager of a farmer's co-operative at the far end of the Moffat Road in Craig. He was a strapping politician with a stubborn streak tempered by a jovial manner. He

seemed to be Billy Adams all over again in his homespun con-
servatism and confidence that Colorado's current population of
one million could handle its own problems. He was skeptical of
the new president in Washington, Franklin D. Roosevelt and his
New Deal program to alleviate the depression, but as the bread-
lines in Denver lengthened and a third of the state's banks
closed their doors, Johnson realized that this crisis could not be
met by conservative methods, such as balancing the budget at
the expense of the needy. All the volunteer relief agencies were
running out of funds, including Denver's Unemployed Citizens
League, which had been handing out a variety of part-time jobs
from the old winter quarters of the Sells-Floto Circus. Reluctantly Johnson turned to the New Deal for help and he asked
the general assembly—nicknamed "the Twiddling Twenty-
Ninth"—to assume some responsibility for the destitute by raising taxes so that Colorado could qualify for federal relief funds.
His request for taxes resulted eventually in the state's first Department of Public Welfare and a system of old-age pensions.

The federal funds that the governor needed were controlled
unofficially by Colorado's Democratic senator in Washington,
Edward P. Costigan, whom Roosevelt selected to guide him on
New Deal programs and their personnel in Colorado. (The other
senator, Billy Adams's nephew Alva B., kept himself pretty
much in the background.) To men like Johnson, Costigan was a
dangerous radical who praised labor unions and the League of
Nations, and who argued that Colorado had obligations beyond
its borders because other states used the waters of its rivers and
because a third of it was federal land owned by all Americans.

Costigan, a small, frail man who suffered from asthma, was
born in Virginia and educated at Harvard. He had held unpopular views since the turn of the century when, as a young
Denver lawyer, he had accepted Theodore Roosevelt's thesis
that the public domain of the West was a national trust. He ran
twice for governor unsuccessfully as a Bull Moose progressive,
turned Democrat to support Woodrow Wilson, and spent ten

years in Washington as a Wilson appointee on the U. S. Tariff Commission. He thought that low tariffs would increase international trade and discourage wars, and he enraged the Colorado beet-sugar people by proposing to reduce the duty on cane sugar imported from Cuba. The ranchers detested him because he favored grazing fees on public land and because he had backed Enos Mills in the Rocky Mountain National Park fight. Nobody was surprised when he returned to Denver in 1928 to become general counsel for that other dangerous radical Josephine Roche and her Rocky Mountain Fuel Company. Miss Roche had horrified the business community by coming to terms with the United Mine Workers.

When Costigan ran for the U. S. Senate in 1930, his program for federal aid brought him a landslide victory. He won the solid support of debt-ridden farmers and unemployed workers, and of the state's Spanish-Americans, who found him attractive partly because he was only half Anglo. (His mother was Spanish.) Through the worst years of the depression—1932 to 1936—he worked hard to keep things moving smoothly. Among his problems were Johnson's jealousy of his authority and the running feud which the governor carried on with Roosevelt's relief administrator in Washington, Harry Hopkins. But Costigan's health broke down completely in 1936. This misfortune forced his retirement and his replacement in the Senate by Johnson. Thus ended the career of a courageous and farsighted man who devoted a great deal of his time to defending the public domain in Colorado against those who urged its unrestricted exploitation however destructive of the land.

The Colorado programs of the New Deal unfolded rapidly under Franklin D. Roosevelt, accompanied by heated debates as to whether they were accomplishing anything. The debates were mostly politics. Progress was being made. The Silver Purchase Act of 1934 and the rise in the price paid by the government for gold from twenty to thirty-five dollars an ounce revived mining

in Cripple Creek and other ghost camps. Swarms of unemployed young men found instructive work in the Civilian Conservation Corps under the direction of army officers. This remarkable program was perfectly adapted to the state with its
vast forest reserves. The workers, enrolled for six months in
batches of one hundred and seventy-five members, built roads
and trails, fought forest fires, and contoured the hillsides to stop
erosion.

The federal programs could not avert tragedies that came to
the dry-land farmers of the eastern plains who had been expos-
ing their fields to the winds by excessive plowing ever since the
boom days of World War I. The soil stayed put when crops
were coming up during wet years, but four years of drouth
began in 1931. With nothing growing, "black blizzards"—
seven or eight of these spells of high wind might descend on a
farm in one summer—could pick up the exposed topsoil and
carry it as far away as Denver and Pueblo, where it would
darken the skies as it drifted down on those cities. Countless
families, particularly in the counties of Baca, Las Animas, and
Prowers in southeastern Colorado, raised nothing at all during
the four-year drouth. Many of them found it hard to bear the
weird, swirling dust, which blotted out the sun, killed their livestock and poultry, seeped into their homes and made breathing
difficult. Instances of insanity and suicide were not uncommon.
Before the drouth ended, half of these farmers abandoned their
ruined property and fled to California or to the pinto-bean
country of the western slope. Those who stayed on were supported by funds paid to them by the Agricultural Adjustment
Administration for not planting wheat or for practicing soil conservation.

Of all Colorado programs, by far the most successful were
those financed after 1935 by the Works Progress Administration, usually under the sponsorship of local agencies. Tens of
thousands of Coloradans were put to work in a wide range of
WPA projects, nearly a hundred in all. During those years nine

thousand miles of state highways were constructed or improved. Sewage plants and waterworks were modernized. Hundreds of schools, gymnasiums, and other public structures were built—a library at Greeley, a swimming pool at Fort Morgan, a town hall at Center, a bridge in Pueblo leading across a lake to the Mineral Palace, stone linings for flood control on Monument Creek at Colorado Springs.

Unemployed Coloradans who practiced the arts for a living were surprised to find that the WPA had use for their crafts. While opponents of the New Deal called such peculiar work "boondoggles," fine painters like Frank Mechau and Boardman Robinson, Archie Musick and Allen True created murals on regional themes to brighten the state's post offices, hospitals, and schools. Groups of artists assembled traveling exhibitions, which were displayed at military posts. In the state museum in Denver, dioramas were produced on the history of transportation in Colorado and on its cattle industry. WPA researchers indexed museum papers and photos and made displays of Clovis points and sea shells. Down near Platteville, historians reconstructed Fort Vasquez, the adobe trading post of the 1830s that had stood on the trail between Bent's Fort and Fort Laramie.

The WPA writers' project hired talented men like Thomas Hornsby Ferril and George Willison to put together the excellent Colorado guidebook based on materials collected throughout the state by roving reporters.[1] Other writers prepared texts for historical plaques and for pamphlets on many subjects—race relations in Denver, how to cook venison, the origin of the oyster bar at Elitch Gardens. But the WPA's music project had troubles. The federally financed Colorado Symphony Orchestra was opposed bitterly by Denver's Civic Symphony on the grounds that the seventy-two musicians of the WPA orchestra were paid more than the private group. A compromise was reached, and the federals performed mainly outside of Denver.

1. *Colorado: A Guide to the Highest State* (New York: Hastings House, 1941).

Though the thirties were sad years for the eastern dry-landers, Coloradans elsewhere did not fare too badly. The state as a whole was not an industrial society. Most residents were not dependent on factory jobs. In the Front Range towns and westerly—Grand Junction, Montrose, Durango, Alamosa—residents cut expenses and lived comfortably if frugally. Frugal living was not depressing when one could enjoy a stimulating climate and spacious mountains at no expense.

There were helpful private developments. Large endowments for public benefits appeared as wealthy Coloradans set up foundations with self-perpetuating boards of trustees so that their estates would not be reduced by inheritance taxes imposed by the socialistic New Deal regime. The eight-million-dollar Bonfils Foundation began in 1933 with the death of Fred Bonfils, the strange, waspish co-owner of *The Denver Post*. The family of Charles Boettcher created the Boettcher Foundation, based on beet-sugar refineries, cement factories, and ranches. In Colorado Springs Spencer Penrose, whose fortune embraced major holdings in Kennecott Copper Corporation and a host of Pikes Peak tourist properties, established El Pomar Foundation just before his death in 1939. The income from El Pomar would be devoted mainly to building and aiding hospitals, libraries, schools, and colleges throughout the state.

Hard times inspired the well-to-do with a yearning for culture to cause a revival on a larger scale of cultural interests that had been displayed thirty years earlier by some of the state's women in promoting Mesa Verde National Park. One of these yearners during the depression was Anne Evans of Denver, the youngest child of Colorado's second territorial governor. She had been born in England in 1871 while John Evans's wife, Margaret, was visiting there. Miss Evans had seen a lot of culture in Europe, and it irked her that Denver seemed to be prouder of its National Western Stock Show than of its historical heritage and its achievements in the arts.

One of Anne Evans's best friends, Ida Kruse McFarlane,

taught English at the University of Denver and was part-owner of the Central City Opera House, which had known glory as the loveliest theater west of Chicago in its mountain pocket above Denver. The theater was falling apart from disuse as the two women developed a plot to shake Denver out of its cowtown boorishness while taking the minds of people off the depression. The result of their plotting was the polite extortion by them of money from members of Denver society to refurbish the opera house and to stage the first performance of the Central City Festival on July 16, 1932, starring the ineffable Lillian Gish in *Camille*. From then on, the summer festival attracted audiences from all over the world to enjoy its operas and plays, to say nothing of the gold camp's earthier amusements in the way of saloons, music halls, square dances and the famous "Face on the Barroom Floor," which Herndon Davis painted one convivial evening in the Teller House.

Among Miss Evans's contributors to the festival were Mrs. Spencer Penrose and Mrs. Meredith Hare of Colorado Springs, both of whom had been encouraging the finer things of life at Pikes Peak for years. Mrs. Penrose had founded the Broadmoor Art Academy in her own home in 1919 with an impressive faculty, including such luminaries as Randall Davey of Santa Fe and George Bellows and Boardman Robinson of New York. While Lillian Gish was packing the opera house at Central City, Mrs. Hare was discussing a new library for Colorado College with Alice Bemis Taylor, whose family had moved to Colorado Springs from Boston in the 1880s and had lavished gifts on the college ever since. It occurred to Mrs. Hare and, through her, to Mrs. Penrose that the Broadmoor Art Academy was a second-rate building for such a first-rate art school, particularly in view of Anne Evans's spectacular Central City Festival, which indicated that Colorado Springs was not keeping pace with the cultural Joneses to the north.

The two women called on Mrs. Taylor, who came to agree with them that a proper art-school facility was more important to the Pikes Peak region than a library. Boardman Robinson was asked to prepare a list of ideas for an art school. He elaborated his list into a free community center—the second of its kind in the United States—where all the arts could be enjoyed—music, ballet, painting, sculpture, drama. The result was the Colorado Springs Fine Arts Center paid for by Mrs. Taylor at a cost of $1,200,000. It was designed by her son-in-law John Gaw Meem of Santa Fe, an innovative architect who gave the center a new kind of monolithic concrete design. It was opened to the public in 1936, and it remains one of the handsomest buildings in the Rockies.

Edward Taylor of Glenwood Springs (no relation to Alice) had served his district in Washington since 1909 and was responsible, in 1921, for persuading Congress to change the name of Grand River to Colorado River. As the venerable chairman of the public-lands committee in the House, Taylor had waited for the right moment to get Congress to do something about some four hundred million acres of federal land in ten western states—land that most people didn't know existed and which was being used free of charge and supervision by stockmen and by companies looking for oil, gas, coal, uranium, and so on. This forgotten empire, larger than all the Eastern-seaboard states put together, was under the jurisdiction of the General Land Office, a moribund and autonomous division of the Department of the Interior. It was all that remained of the original public domain—unwatered, barren land that nobody had claimed because it appeared to have no economic value to speak of—no value to homesteaders or to the Forest Service, Park Service, Bureau of Reclamation, or any other federal institution.

Seven and a half million acres of the land lay in western Colorado—much of it rolling sage country in Moffat, Rio Blanco, Mesa, and Montrose counties. Other Colorado areas were south of Gunnison, in Middle Park, and around Canon City. Congressman Taylor believed that these wastelands had potential value for which those using them should pay fees. The fees would be used partly to improve the land with wells and stock ponds, to stop overgrazing, and to classify the sections so that they could be managed according to their agricultural and mineral promise. When the New Deal arrived, Taylor felt that the time had come to push his grazing bill. He knew that he would be supported by the Secretary of the Interior, the elderly, pepperish Chicagoan named Harold Ickes, who was grasping for all the power in sight. Taylor's bill provided that the four hundred million acres would be taken from the jurisdiction of the General Land Office and placed under Ickes's direct control.

And so it happened. On June 28, 1934, Congress passed the Taylor Grazing Act, in effect ending homesteading forever. Secretary Ickes had gained his empire. All he needed was someone to work out its administration. As it happened, Ed Taylor was lunching now and then with an old friend Farrington Carpenter, a Colorado lawyer who was in Washington lobbying for the cattle industry. In 1907 Carpenter had homesteaded in the Yampa Valley near Hayden and had organized schools there so that bachelor cowboys could find wives among the young girls whom he lured from the East to teach in the schools. (He married one himself.) Through the ensuing years he had spent much of his time as a lawyer setting up grazing areas in Routt National Forest to the satisfaction of rival cattle and sheep outfits with grazing permits.

Though Carpenter was a Republican, Taylor introduced him to Secretary Ickes, who liked his qualifications as a rancher. In a matter of weeks President Roosevelt appointed him to be director of the Interior Department's new division of grazing as prescribed by the Taylor Grazing Act, with an annual salary of $6,500 and a staff of seventeen men borrowed from the U. S. Geological Survey to determine where the grazing lands were. That was no easy task since the only plats for them were scattered in twenty-four western land offices.

This first grazing director was a tolerant, humorous, forthright man with a passion for cowboy shirts, loud ties, and red galluses. He knew the prejudices and problems of stockmen inside and out. For two years he drove his Model-A Ford all over Colorado and the other western states explaining fees, grazing permits, and classifications to thousands of hostile ranchers. Carpenter refused to follow Ickes's suggestion that final approval for grazing permits should rest with officials of the Interior Department in Washington, explaining acidly to the secretary, "Those fellows back East don't know which end of a cow gets up first."

Carpenter vested all authority for his division in local advisory boards of ten men—five cowmen and five sheepmen. These boards laid out grazing districts (five in Colorado) and set grazing fees (five cents a month for a cow, one cent for a sheep). The local autonomy system allayed suspicion among ranchmen and brought the director majority support for a controversial program.[2] But Harold Ickes did not approve of the local boards, which, he said, did not require stockmen to vote the Democratic ticket and which gave them too much power. Eventually Carpenter got tired of Ickes's complaints and resigned his office. But the division that he pioneered continued until 1946, when it was consolidated with the General Land Office into the Bureau of Land Management.

In pushing his grazing act through Congress, Ed Taylor had the larger future of Colorado in mind—a future to be enriched by applying modern science to the fuller development of the state's limited resources. At this time Charles Hansen, editor of *The Greeley Tribune,* was cluttering his ancient rolltop desk with engineering plans for a far more complicated scheme of development that he had been researching for years. Hansen, who looked like a typical preoccupied newsroom man—shirt-sleeves, green eyeshade, black headline crayon behind an ear—had

2. Farrington R. Carpenter, "Range Stockmen Meet the Government," *Denver Westerners Brand Book, 1967* (Denver: Denver Westerners, 1968), pp. 329–353.

added the duties of New Deal relief chairman for Weld County to his editing and scheming. The depression soup kitchens in Greeley appalled him. So did the reports of despair down the South Platte—despair and bankruptcy caused by the drouth-created shortage of water in the irrigation ditches that nourished the farms all the way east to Julesburg. In June of 1933, an official of the Public Works Administration wrote to him for ideas to put men to work in his relief area. Hansen outlined his development scheme and sent it to Washington by return mail. The scheme would be known later as the Colorado-Big Thompson Project, the largest transmountain diversion of water for irrigation and power ever attempted.

The man who would come to be called "the godfather of the Big T" faced obstacles as formidable as the Continental Divide that blocked him from the western-slope streams that he hoped to exploit. The Colorado traditions of self-reliance and distrust of the federal government were strong in Weld County, which was populated by descendants of Greeley's Union Colony pioneers and a mixed bag of thrifty Swedes, Russo-Germans, Poles, and Pennsylvania Dutch. Hansen was asked how he had the nerve to offer a plan to grow more irrigated crops when the Agricultural Adjustment Administration was paying farmers to grow less. And what made him think that the people of the western slope could spare any of the water from the Colorado River and its tributaries on which they depended totally? It was pointed out that the Colorado River Compact had gone into effect in 1929, requiring that the seven Colorado River states divide the flow among themselves according to their needs. The needs were enormous, particularly those of the metropolises of Los Angeles and Phoenix, and yet the Colorado was a small river compared to the Missouri and Snake and Columbia. By the terms of the compact, the ranchers and farmers of Colorado's sparsely populated western slope found themselves reduced to half the volume of irrigation water that they had always regarded as theirs. To cut the volume further to please Charles Hansen and the South

Platte valley crowd was unthinkable. The western slopers were not to blame that Weld County had too many farmers or that the South Platte was not really a river but just a creek.

The would-be water robber persevered. He added power plants to his plans—hydroelectric plants that would produce cheap electricity for Greeley and Fort Collins, Loveland and Longmont. Eastern-slope newspapers cheered him on, and so did the railroads and beet-sugar refiners. He was supported in Congress by a lobby of manufacturers of all the machines and materials required to make such a system. He organized the promotional Northern Colorado Water Users Association headed by himself and composed of leaders of the prairie counties of the South Platte—leaders representing some six thousand growers of sugar beets and potatoes, beans, corn, fruit, alfalfa, poultry, eggs, hogs, and cattle. This group became the Northern Colorado Water Conservancy District (Charles Hansen, president), which was authorized by the state legislature to sign construction contracts with the U. S. Bureau of Reclamation and to manage the water diversion after it was completed.

The indefatigable editor answered the objections of conservationists by promising that the Big T would evolve in such a way as not to disfigure the scenery or disturb wildlife. His biggest obstacle was the opposition of the Western Slope Protective Association chaired by Congressman Ed Taylor. But Hansen could reason with Taylor, who was a boyhood friend of his. The two had worked together as cub reporters chasing fire engines and ambulances for *The Grand Rapids Herald* back in Michigan. Taylor and his group decided to drop their opposition when Hansen put into his plans the huge Green Mountain Reservoir near Kremmling on the Blue River branch of the Colorado. Water would pile up in this western-slope reservoir during the heavy spring runoff to more than compensate the farms downstream for the waters upstream that would be diverted eastward.

Many anxious months passed, but the great day for Charles Hansen finally arrived. On December 21, 1937, President Roosevelt signed the bill authorizing an initial appropriation of $900,000 so that the Bureau of Reclamation could start work on the Big T to bring 300,000 extra acre-feet of western-slope water annually—a thirty percent increase—to the existing ditches of the South Platte valley. In essence, this phantasmagoria of a plot to make nature conform to Hansen's idea of what was best for everybody was based first on building what would be the largest man-made lake in the state, Granby Reservoir in Middle Park, where runoff from branches of the Colorado would be stored. This Granby water would be lifted by pumps into the smaller Shadow Mountain Reservoir. From Shadow Mountain it would flow into the popular yachting center Grand Lake, where a 13.1-mile tunnel would carry it under Rocky Mountain National Park and the Continental Divide to the eastern-slope exit portal and Big Thompson River near Estes Park village. The flow of water from Shadow Mountain would be regulated to keep Grand Lake (and yachts) at a near-constant level regardless of the volume being drawn off in the tunnel. There was an infinitude of ramifications to the original primary purpose of irrigation—power plants, transmission lines, conduits, syphons. Dams and reservoirs and tunnels on the eastern slope would serve to bring the water to the irrigation ditches of South Platte tributaries. The projected main tunnel was named in honor of Senator Alva B. Adams, who had pushed the first appropriation bill through Congress. The naming was deplored by many people who thought that it should be called the Charles Hansen Tunnel.

The Big T was supposed to cost $44,000,000 and to be completed in five years. The total bill was $169,000,000 and its maze of facilities was not operating fully until the mid-1950s. The long delay was caused by an event that occurred on December 7, 1941. It constituted an international catastrophe that would bring changes to the state at least as profound as those which came with the gold rush of 1859, the railroads in 1870, and the automobile at the turn of the century.

10

War and Peace

$\mathcal{C}$OLORADO was a sluggish community in December 1941, when Pearl Harbor was attacked and the United States declared war on Japan. The citizens had survived the depression, but their future looked unpromising and they had no particular incentive to improve matters. The state's population had been stalled at a million or so for a decade. The assessed valuation of its private property was a third less than it had been in 1930. Many of its young people had gone away to make careers elsewhere. No investment capital appeared to be coming in from the East.

But there were some hopeful signs before Pearl Harbor—if improvement induced by war can be called "hopeful." A federal arms factory was under construction in Denver. Plans had been approved to build a chemical-warfare plant called the Rocky Mountain Arsenal north of Aurora. A trio of Colorado Springs businessmen, Russell Law, Douglas Jardine, and H. Chase Stone, had collected a pot of $28,000 from the city's chamber of commerce to finance a desperate assault on congressmen and army officials in Washington. The Pikes Peak group was lobbying for a modest training camp costing a million or two on a five-thousand-acre tract of prairie land south of town, which the city was willing to give to the army free.

170

The assault was desperate because the tourist and health business of Colorado Springs (population, 30,000) had dwindled disastrously and might vanish entirely under gas rationing and other wartime restrictions. The lobbyists roamed Washington loaded down with charts and studies to show how cheap it would be to train a GI in the bracing climate of Pikes Peak and how easy it would be for the army to find housing in a resort with fifteen hundred homes empty and for rent. When Washington officials displayed interest in the possibilities at Pikes Peak, they were sent to the city's official host, Charles L. Tutt, president of the Broadmoor, who gave them tender care in the hotel. After their working hours of inspection, those weary officials who needed refreshment were introduced to the pre-Volstead Act treasures of the Broadmoor's creator, the late Spencer Penrose, who had had the wisdom to lay away a few carloads of French wines and Scotch whiskey before Prohibition became law in 1919. Much of this stock was still in storage at the hotel when the onset of World War II began to prevent such delectable imports from reaching the United States.

On December 29, 1941, Colorado Springs was awarded its army installation, to be called Camp Carson in honor of the old trapper and trader Kit Carson who had guided John Charles Frémont around the Front Range region in the 1840s. But Camp Carson was nothing like the modest post that the chamber of commerce men had visualized. Congress appropriated thirty million dollars just to start off. (The assessed valuation of Colorado Springs in 1941 was twenty-eight million.) The camp would extend far south of the gift tract to cover some sixty thousand acres. It was to be populated by thirty-seven thousand soldiers, three thousand mules and horses, platoons of police dogs, and a few thousand prisoners of war. It would have a 6,500-acre subsidiary called Camp Hale for training the proposed Tenth Mountain Infantry Division, a pioneer unit in cold-weather survival and military skiing. Camp Hale would be built at an old sawmill site called Pando on a bulge of Eagle River (*pando* means "bulge" in Spanish) just over the Continental Divide north of Leadville.

The reactivated 89th Infantry Division moved into Camp Carson in midsummer of 1942. Thereafter, the nation's military leaders seemed determined to overwhelm the Pikes Peak region with federal largesse. Ent Air Force Base was established that year in Colorado Springs, and the municipal airport became Peterson Field, where bombing squadrons were trained. (The name was in memory of Lt. Edward J. Peterson, who died at the field in a crash of a P-38.) Ent evolved into CONAD (Continental Air Defense Command), and in 1957 CONAD became NORAD (North American Air Defense Command), a command post of indescribable complexity for the joint defense against air attack of the United States and Canada. NORAD was the nerve center where commanding generals received reports from three hundred and fifty aircraft-detection points scattered throughout the northern hemisphere. In 1966 it was moved for safety's sake into a vast hole bored into the south end of Cheyenne Mountain at a cost of $150 million. This Combat Operations Center—nicknamed "the Cave"—consists today of three three-story buildings sitting on vibration-proof springs, eight smaller structures, a power plant, and a big water-storage area. Here two thousand specialists in communications manage a vast array of electronic brains, sensors, and tracking systems to guard the air space of two nations.

Long before NORAD arrived, Colorado Springs had lost its forlorn, empty-bed look and was drowning in prosperity brought by Camp Carson. The rattlesnakes and jackrabbits that had inhabited the prairie bordering the town had fled. The land was covered with housing developments, built or frantically abuilding. The undermanned Colorado Springs police department tried hard to maintain a semblance of law and order among the frolicsome young GIs from Carson and their girls out for a good time on Saturday nights. And even as residents wondered what had happened to the place they had known a decade earlier as Little

London—signifying refinement and repose—the city's boosters were at it again. This time they aimed to convince the U. S. Air Force that Colorado Springs was the best place for its proposed Air Force Academy, which Congress had authorized early in 1954.

It seemed to be the most impossible of dreams. Colorado Springs could hardly expect to win this plum of military plums on top of the two huge institutions—$400 million worth of them—that it had received already. Four hundred other cities had squads of buttonholers in Washington equally loaded down with bales of convincing charts. And still the Pikes Peakers lobbied away. Perhaps they hoped that President Dwight Eisenhower would endorse their petition. The president's wife had grown up in Denver, and he had spent much time fly-fishing on the trout streams of the state. One of his golf partners, Governor Dan Thornton, had induced the Colorado legislature to budget a million dollars with which to buy land for the academy.

In the late spring of 1954, Colonel Charles Lindbergh and the rest of the Air Force Academy selection committee reduced its list of possible sites to three—Alton, Illinois; Lake Geneva, Wisconsin; and Colorado Springs. And then the impossible came to pass. On June 15, 1954, a 17,500-acre site north of Colorado Springs was designated for the new service institution. Four years later the first cadets moved into that shining center of steel, aluminum, glass, and marble poised on a buttresslike mesa spreading away from the Rampart Range. Four-lane highways curved through the pines of the area, tying the campus and football stadium to communities for faculty and service personnel. Today the $200 million academy draws more visitors than any other single attraction in the Rocky Mountains.

While Colorado Springs struggled to adjust to the academy, to a permanent Fort Carson (1954) in place of Camp Carson, and to a civilian population that would increase from 30,000 to more than 200,000, the rest of Colorado was growing also with the benign aid of federal money. Water began flowing to farms of the South Platte valley through the Alva B. Adams Tunnel of the Big T in 1946. Agriculture flourished generally as dry-land farmers, remembering the dust bowl, took better care of their topsoil. The navy established Buckley Field in Denver in 1942. Lowry Field for training aerial photographers was enlarged, along with the Denver Mint, U. S. Customs House, and Fitzsimons Hospital. In the late 1940s the Denver Arms Plant was converted into Denver Federal Center, an immense grouping of bureaucracies where workers in a thousand offices handled a staggering variety of government services. Meanwhile, the nearby city of Boulder prospered with the arrival of a branch of the National Bureau of Standards, the National Center for Atmospheric Research, and the increase of student enrollment at the University of Colorado by 1950 to ten thousand students, more than the total college enrollment in Colorado a decade earlier.

The propinquity of training camps, airfields, and intelligence units like The Cave at Pikes Peak attracted to the Front Range cities a host of ultramodern enterprises such as Martin Marietta Corporation and Sunstrand Corporation (aerospace plants) in Denver; Ball Brothers Research Corporation (orbiting solar observatories) in Boulder; and Hewlett Packard Company (electronic measuring equipment) and Kaman Sciences Corporation (nuclear physics research), both in Colorado Springs. The Federal Railroad Administration established a High Speed Ground Test Center near Pueblo. At Rocky Flats between Denver and Boulder, a plant was built for the Atomic Energy Commission to treat plutonium for use in devices designed to blow up the world if necessary. Assurances by the AEC that nothing radioactively or explosively dangerous was going on at Rocky Flats did not dispel the anxiety of residents in the area.

World War II produced one mining triumph with so little fanfare that few Coloradans were impressed by it. Back in 1879 when Horace Tabor was riding high, a promoter named Charles Senter staked a presumed gold-ore claim near Leadville on Fremont Pass (11,318 feet) adjoining Bartlett Mountain. The ore was identified later as molybdenum, and the Climax Molybdenum Company (American Metal Climax Incorporated, today) was formed to meet a modest demand for the metal in light-bulb filaments. In the 1920s, steel makers back East tried it to harden their product with excellent results. During World War II, huge amounts of such hardened steel were needed for many kinds of armament. Molybdenum production from Bartlett Mountain leaped to twenty-eight million pounds in a single war year. Today half the world's molybdenum comes from this extraordinary rock pile two and a half miles above sea level. The mountain appears to be composed of solid molybdenum ore. The value of its recent output—averaging $120 million annually—far exceeds the total value of all the gold and silver mined in Colorado during peak years of the nineteenth century.

The rise of molybdenum was a one-company, one bonanza affair. It was attended in the 1940s and 1950s by the uranium craze, described by Al Look in his book *U-Boom* as "the most fabulous mineral hunt and stock-selling spree in all history." [1] Since the start, in 1941, of the Manhattan Project to develop the atomic bomb, army engineers had been buying ore from the old carnotite dumps of Paradox Valley. The concentrate of the dumps had been used in Paris by Pierre and Marie Curie in their research on radioactivity at the turn of the century. But the big uranium-buying program did not begin until 1948, when the Atomic Energy Commission enlarged the wartime mill at Grand Junction and issued an appeal for uranium ore at high prices with which to build a stockpile of atomic bombs. The rush started almost overnight, resembling in its intensity the gold rush of 1859—thousands upon thousands of greenhorn prospectors from every walk of life and from every part of the nation hurrying to the Colorado Plateau region of the western slope, eyes shining with visions of enormous wealth. But their equip-

1. Al Look, *U-Boom* (Denver: Bell Press, 1956), p. iii.

ment was not the pick, burro, and frying pan combination of yesteryear. The modern miners traveled in jeeps and trucks, prop planes and helicopters, and they carried Geiger counters, which clicked in response to gamma rays given off by radioactive uranium under their feet as they scrambled about the lonely, arid canyons of the Dolores and San Miguel river country. At night, many of them lodged in frenzied settlements like Uravan and Naturita, Paradox and Bedrock, jamming the restaurants and bars and sleeping five in a bed if they could find one.

A few of them did find fortunes during those years before the federal purchase program was reduced in 1958. But the majority emerged with nothing to show for their toil except memories of the strange, wild beauty of the uranium region with its weird rock formations in rainbow colors and its gorgeous sunrises and sunsets. The uranium of Colorado is still very much in demand, but the mining of it has settled down to the unadventurous routine of corporate enterprise. The state's annual production in the $16 million range is used mainly in the nuclear reactors of utility companies.

As we have seen, the destinies of Colorado were often shaped by happy accidents. One of these occurred late in 1941 when the army picked Pando north of Leadville as the site for Camp Hale, where the Tenth Mountain Division would be trained. The idea of the Tenth Mountain had originated soon after the cold-weather invasion of Finland by the Russians and the German invasion of Norway in the early stages of World War II. These ominous events had caused General George Marshall to listen seriously to officials of the civilian National Ski Patrol who argued that military use should be made of the skills of American skiers to counteract the growing numbers of combat skiers in enemy armies abroad.

Members of the 87th Mountain Infantry, core regiment of the projected new division, began arriving at Camp Hale in the fall of 1942. At an altitude of 9,480 feet above sea level, Camp

Hale was a rough place for many of the recruits who were unused to high altitudes, deep snow, and bitter winter weather. To recover from frostbite and a coughing affliction called "Pando hack," some of the trainees would repair, on weekends, to the lower altitude and milder temperatures of a quaint Victorian village of a few hundred residents, the once-booming silver town of Aspen. Here they found comfort in the Jerome Hotel, which Jerome Wheeler had built in 1889. Wheeler had sold it to a Syrian bartender Mansor Elisha, whose son Laurence was managing the hotel in the 1940s. The bar of the Jerome had a soda fountain which the hard-liquor skiers from Camp Hale scorned until they discovered the magic that accrued to a chocolate milkshake if it were spiced with one or two or perhaps three jiggers of Kentucky bourbon. This unique health drink became standard thereafter under the name "Aspen crud." Those who imbibed a few felt fortified for the scary trip in a boat-and-rope conveyance to the top of Corkscrew ski run on the lower slopes of Ajax Mountain. The boat crept jerkily upward under the power of an ancient gasoline engine. Sometimes it reached the top of the run and sometimes the rope broke or the engine died or the boat rolled over. In such cases the passengers jumped for their lives.

The Tenth Mountain finished training and left Camp Hale to fight the Germans in Italy, but the boat was still at Aspen on a bright morning in May 1945, when Mr. and Mrs. Walter Paepcke of Chicago arrived at the Jerome, partly out of curiosity to see the Elk Mountains and partly because they had saved up enough gasoline-ration coupons for the trip through Leadville from their eastern-slope ranch. The town was quiet. During their brief stay, the two visitors looked at the scene from different points of view. Walter Paepcke, the business genius who had founded the hugely successful Container Corporation of America in 1926, wondered what could be done to make a paying proposition out of such an attractive semighost town. Elizabeth Paepcke, an ardent conservationist, fell in love with the forested hills and the crystal beauty of the Roaring Fork River. She had heard of conservation first as a child in her native Baltimore from an old family friend Gifford Pinchot. She had learned more about it during vacations at Longs Peak, where Enos Mills had enthralled her with his talk of birds and flowers, mushrooms and butterflies, and the need to protect Estes by creating Rocky Mountain National Park.

In the golden fall of 1945, the Paepckes drove again to Aspen to set up a small firm, the Aspen Company, involving the restoration of gingerbread homes and a long lease on the Jerome Hotel. Paepcke had been studying the nation's ski industry—mainly overcrowded resorts in the low mountains of New England where it could snow hard and rain hard on the same midwinter day. Skiing was not unknown in Colorado, but its followers were few. There was a ski jump, vintage 1912, at Steamboat Springs, a practice slope which had been used by the Tenth Mountain near Leadville, a few runs at Pikes Peak, and several around Denver laid out by the Arlberg Ski Club. Many motorists seemed to be afraid of the high country in any season—afraid of the altitude, of avalanches, of shelf roads, of electrical storms.

An expert European skier André Roch had been praising the Aspen terrain long before the Tenth Mountain became fond of the Corkscrew run. On an impulse, Paepcke sent some engineers up Ajax Mountain to see if a modern chair lift would suit it. They reported favorably, so he bought a lift—cost, $250,000. It was opened on January 10, 1947. Since it was the longest—three miles—and fastest lift in the world at the time, it drew lowlanders from all over the West just to look at it—and to launch the great Rocky Mountain ski boom.

The Paepckes did not rouse Aspen from half a century of lethargy all by themselves. As World War II ended, they had the help of the best skiers in the Tenth Mountain—men hurrying back to the powder snow of the Colorado Rockies after dreaming about its ski slopes through the Italian campaign. The former Austrian champion Friedl Pfeifer took over as head of Paepcke's Aspen Ski School. Steve Knowlton, once a leading collegiate skier, arrived on the Roaring Fork to race downhill by day and run an Aspen night spot after dark. Fritz Benedict settled down as a gifted architect and developer of homes on Red Mountain. Dozens of Tenth Mountain members hung around Ajax Mountain as ski bums, adding color and skiing excellence to the scene before moving on to complete the development of the state as a winter sports region. Gordon Wren returned to his native Steamboat Springs to expand facilities at Howelsen Hill. Larry Jump started the sport at Arapahoe Basin. Paul Duke wound up at Breckenridge. Leon Wilmot became director of Ski Broadmoor in Colorado Springs. Merrill Hastings founded a ski magazine in Denver. Stuart Mace set up a sled-dog farm at Ashcroft near Aspen. Peter Seibert and an ex-uranium prospector Earl Eaton began planning the recreation phenomenon of the 1960s, the town of Vail in the Gore Range.

It was characteristic of Walter Paepcke, who had started it all, to want to expand a project as soon as it had succeeded. A winter sports resort was fine, but there was Aspen's summer overhead to worry about. In the fall of 1947, Paepcke mentioned his problem to friends at the University of Chicago, Chancellor Robert M. Hutchins and Mortimer Adler, a professor of humanities who was teaching The Fat Man's Club of leading Chicago tycoons how to bridge the gap between their world of commerce and the world of the spirit. Hutchins proposed a cultural summer at Aspen, a kind of Salzburg in America with a program spectacular enough to lure people into the hinterlands. Adler, in his turn, suggested an Aspen version of the educational Fat Man's Club with embellishments to improve the health of the businessmen as well as their minds.

Paepcke leaped to both challenges. He staged his Goethe Festival honoring the 200th anniversary of the birth of the German poet during the summer of 1949. His program in a huge orange tent in Aspen Meadows included lectures by Dr. Albert

Schweitzer and Thornton Wilder, concerts by the Minneapolis Symphony, and recitals by platoons of musicians—Gregor Piatigorsky, Artur Rubenstein, Nathan Milstein, Erica Morini and many others. A year later, Paepcke opened the Aspen Institute for Humanistic Studies—the University of Denver took it over in 1976—as an addition to his music festival. Mortimer Adler conducted the Great Books program for groups of business executives. Between Adler's lectures on Aristotle and Thoreau, John Stuart Mill and Karl Marx, the executives took up body building in Paepcke's Aspen Health Center.

From 1945 until his death in 1961, Paepcke and his wife contributed a million dollars to their dream of Aspen as an international center of culture and recreation. Thereafter, the Paepcke idea was applied up and down the Roaring Fork. The communities of Aspen Highlands and Snowmass Village were built, offering year-round recreation. Such rapid growth would bring problems to the Elk Mountain environment in time, but the cultural programs of Aspen itself continued with the same flair that the Paepckes had given to them in the beginning.

As the population of Colorado moved steadily upward from 1940 on, some residents found themselves disturbed by a suspicion that the state was heading for trouble in the distribution of its water. How long would there be enough of it to go around at the present rate of growth? The eastern slope, where eighty percent of the people lived, was full of plans for taking water from the western slope—that is, from Colorado River. The eastern slope had no water of its own worth mentioning. The flow of the South Platte was one-tenth the volume of the Colorado; the Arkansas one-fifteenth. The Big T diversion had seemed to help the South Platte. But as the cost of the Big T had skyrocketed, its power production had to be enlarged to produce more revenue. The cheap power that was produced had stimulated the industrial growth—and the water consumption—of metropolitan Denver. To meet this new demand on its limited supply, Denver officials bought water rights on the Blue River branch of the Colorado and planned what would be called Dillon Reservoir and the twenty-three-mile Roberts Tunnel to bring Blue River water to Denver. Meanwhile, Colorado Springs, Aurora, and Pueblo had prepared similar transmountain diversion plans to meet their everincreasing water needs.

In 1949 the seriousness of the problem was accentuated when the states of Colorado, Wyoming, Utah, and New Mexico signed the Colorado River Basin Compact, signifying the decision of the four Upper Basin states to make full use of their half of the total flow of the Colorado River system that had been assigned to them in 1922 by the seven-state Colorado River Compact. The other half of the river's flow of fifteen million acre-feet of water annually had been assigned to the three Lower Basin states, California, Arizona, and Nevada.

Up to that time, the Upper Basin states had developed irrigation and municipal uses for only forty percent of their allotment of seven and a half million acre-feet. The division roughly among themselves was Colorado, fifty-two percent; Utah, twenty-three percent; Wyoming fourteen percent; New Mexico, eleven percent. By contrast to their slow approach, the Lower Basin states had won construction of Hoover Dam in 1936 to irrigate their lands and bring them hydroelectric power—a facility that made it easy for them to use much more than their allotment. The Upper Basin states, therefore, had to increase their needs for water or face a demand from the Lower Basin that they give up their rights to the millions of acre-feet of water that they were not using—a basic rule of water law in the West. To accomplish this end, the Upper Basin group proposed to Congress the Colorado River Storage Project, consisting of ten big dams, most of them in Colorado, to produce irrigation and power, and eleven smaller dams for irrigation alone. Operation of the dams would require use of all the water that had been assigned to the Upper Basin states in 1922.

Out of this proposal a totally unforeseen complication arose.

One of the biggest dams was to be built just below a lovely glade of cottonwoods and watercress called Echo Park at the junction of the Green and Yampa rivers. Echo Park was in the remote center of Dinosaur National Monument at the foot of one of the most dramatic and beautiful river gorges in the nation, the seventeen-mile Lodore Canyon which one of Major Powell's explorers had named after reading Robert Southey's poem, "The Cataract of Lodore." President Wilson had created the monument around a quarry of dinosaur bones in eastern Utah. In 1938, President Roosevelt increased the original eighty acres to 209,000 acres, mostly in the northwest corner of Colorado. Roosevelt's proclamation contained the proviso that no dam or reservoir could be built within the body of the park but only near the north border above the Gates of Lodore in Brown's Park.

The proposed Echo Park dam would be 525 feet high and would flood Lodore Canyon as the water backed up the Green for sixty-three miles and up the canyon of the Yampa for forty-four miles to create a 43,400-acre lake and produce a billion kilowatt hours of electricity annually. To the ranchers and businessmen of the Yampa Valley, the dam would bring cheap power, and they expected it to transform 300,000 acres of desert into farmland. To them, the location seemed ideal for a fluctuating storage reservoir because nobody ever went to what they called "that graveyard of extinct reptiles" except stray artifact hunters. Senator Ed Johnson praised the plan which, he declared, would convert a "menacing and wastrel river" into as great a national resource as Hoover Dam.

With Big Ed behind them, most Coloradans were confident that Congress would approve this dam, and they were surprised that protests arose when the project was announced—protests that grew in volume as the debate went on through the months and then the years of the early 1950s. The protests evolved at last into a national wave of complaint when the Senate passed and sent to the House in the spring of 1955 a bill authorizing

Echo Park dam and five others at a cost of $1.1 billion. The ardor of the protests baffled Senator Joseph O'Mahoney of Wyoming, who declared that a new and fearsome element had entered American politics—an element of people calling themselves "environmentalists" who, living far from the cause of their displeasure, based their views not on common sense and practical economics but on "sentimental and aesthetic feelings." [2]

The senator was quite right to be concerned. What was happening was a campaign by a lobbying group in Washington called the Council of Conservationists representing some fifty organizations—the Sierra Club, Wilderness Society, National Wildlife Federation, and so on. The head of the lobby was Ulysses S. Grant, III, a retired army general of distinguished forebears, whose hobbies were historic preservation and the beautification of cities. General Grant stressed three points in his lobbying—that the dam builders of the Bureau of Reclamation knew the price of everything and the value of nothing; that the federal power acts of 1921 and 1935 forbade power developments in national parks and monuments; and that Echo Park Dam, if permitted, would go on like the Trojan horse to destroy the character of the national park system. These opinions were circulated and applauded far and wide. And, on June 25, 1955, when the House Interior subcommittee sent a less costly version of the Colorado River Storage Project to the full House for a vote, Echo Park Dam was not recommended.

During the sixties and early seventies, Colorado and its thirsty Front Range cities did get a plethora of federal dams, reservoirs, tunnels, and power plants, though enthusiasm for them lessened as complications emerged because of their soaring costs and the damage that they did to river valleys. Two big dams were completed in 1975 on the Gunnison River—Blue

<hr />

2. Joseph O'Mahoney and Ulysses S. Grant, III, "Are You For or Against the Echo Park Dam?" *Collier's* 135:76–82 (18 February 1955).

Mesa and Morrow Point. A third Gunnison dam, Crystal, was partly built. The big Navajo Dam on San Juan River in New Mexico created a reservoir some of which was in Colorado. Construction was proceeding on the Frying Pan–Arkansas transmountain diversion to nourish the city of Pueblo and the irrigated farms of the Arkansas.

These big dams and power plants, plus Flaming Gorge and Glen Canyon in Utah and Fontenelle in Wyoming, had been part of the original Upper Colorado River Project of 1949. They brought to the four-state Upper Basin one of the most heavily subsidized water systems in the world.

But in spite of the dams, water continued to be a problem for the state. That problem, however, was overshadowed in the minds of many by another which was just beginning to show above the horizon.

11

Crossroad

*T*HE admission that the United States faced a critical short-age of fuel to run the most affluent society on earth came in 1973 when President Nixon outlined Project Independence to make the nation self-sufficient in energy. Two years later, President Ford asked Congress to rush the plan along by supplying six billion dollars in guaranteed loans, four and a half billion for price supports on oil and coal, and six hundred million in construction grants. These federal funds, reaching a total of $11.1 billion, were part of an appropriation bill sent to Congress on behalf of the Energy Research and Development Administration. The purpose of the appropriation was to subsidize private companies—mostly Eastern conglomerates and combines of conglomerates—in building an oil shale industry and in more than quadrupling the nation's coal production by 1985.

It was obvious that the brunt of a successful Project Independence would fall on Colorado. The U.S. Geological Survey had estimated that the Colorado Rockies contained seventy-five percent of the nation's shale oil reserves and tens of trillions of tons of coal in convenient areas, which, because of its low content of sulphur, was suitable to use in plants to manufacture gas and as a substitute for oil in driving the generators of electrical utilities. President Ford had indicated his attitude toward the effects of such massive extraction of resources by vetoing two bills passed by Congress to control the strip-mining of coal.

The original ERDA appropriations bill of 1973 and adjusted versions of it were stalled in Congress when 1976 began. But the mere thought of an economic takeover of the state and removal of its mineral wealth by the rest of the country in an effort to solve a national crisis by programs that might or might not work brought Coloradans to a crossroad. It forced them to make up their minds at last about the basic conflict running through their history—the conflict between their wish to preserve their beautiful land for the joy of it and their need to mar its beauty by exploiting its resources for material gain. They had seen already unpleasant changes in their way of life brought by federal spending in the state of two billion dollars or so over thirty years since World War II. Some of the spending had unexpected results, as in the case of irrigation systems that became primarily systems selling hydroelectricity to meet the excessive cost of the systems. What would happen if many times two billions of dollars were dumped on Colorado in a single decade? And the billions would not be spent by Coloradans familiar with this special environment—resident leaders in the style of William Gilpin or John Evans or General Palmer. The money would be spent by out-of-state entities controlled by absentee boards of directors subject to change overnight.

Oil shale in northwestern Colorado is a rock filled with a mineral called kerogen, which becomes a refinable synthetic oil when heated to a temperature of nine hundred degrees Fahrenheit. The oil has the properties of crude oil (petroleum) but it is composed of a different set of hydrocarbons. Shale oil had no commercial value until 1973, when the Arab oil embargo boosted the world price of crude oil to more than ten dollars a barrel. Some experts on shale oil say that their product can compete with crude oil at ten dollars a barrel. Others have put the competitive price far higher—twenty or thirty dollars a barrel.

Oil shale is found over some forty square miles of Colorado's

Book Plateau in Rio Blanco and Garfield counties. The sparsely populated area is marked by sandstone and shale outcrops, and it is covered with scrub oak, juniper, piñon, grass, and sage. The rolling country rises to a divide at around seven thousand feet of altitude. From the divide, creeks drain north into White River near the town of Meeker (population, 1,600). Creeks running south drain into Colorado River near Rifle (population, 2,500). The area was beloved by the White River Ute Indians for its profusion of wild life before the Meeker Massacre of 1879, and it is famous among hunters today for its wild horses, elk, bobcats, and an enormous wintering herd of deer numbering around thirty thousand.

The distance from Rifle on Colorado River to Meeker on White River is forty-two miles. Halfway between them the highway crosses a small west-running stream called Piceance (pronounced "pee-ance"—a Ute word meaning "tall grass.") It was along this creek in 1930 that the nation's richest oil shale deposits were discovered, mostly on federal land that came later under the jurisdiction of the Bureau of Land Management in the Department of the Interior—some 800,000 acres containing an estimated 600 billion barrels of shale oil (the total reserves of *crude* oil in the entire United States are put at a maximum of 400 billion barrels).

In 1972, the Department of the Interior announced that two five-thousand-acre tracts of Piceance oil shale land were ready for leasing as prototypes for the development of the new energy industry. Two years later, according to an article by Sylvia Lewis in *Planning Magazine,* one of the twenty-year leases was purchased for $210 million by Standard Oil of Indiana and Gulf Oil Corporation under the name Rio Blanco Oil Shale Project. The purchase was prompted partly by a tremendous rise in crude-oil prices accompanying the Arab oil embargo. A second lease was sold for $117 million to a combine headed by Atlantic Richfield Company, which had been operating a shale oil pilot plant on Parachute Creek near Rifle for some years. Others in

this second combine—called the Colony Development Operation—were Oil Shale Corporation, Shell Oil Company, and
Ashland Oil Company. It was the plan of the combine to open
in 1978 the nation's first commercial shale oil plant on Piceance
Creek at a cost of $600 million to produce fifty thousand barrels
of synthetic oil a day.[1]

When Congress refused to guarantee loans for private oil
shale development at the start of 1976, Atlantic Richfield and
Oil Shale Corporation withdrew from the Colony plan, putting
construction of the proposed plant in jeopardy. The Rio Blanco
project was suspended also, but smaller companies proposed
operations on Piceance Creek in large enough numbers to draw
predictions from Interior officials that a 500,000-barrel-a-day
production in Colorado was possible by 1985. But many oil
men were less optimistic. They pointed out that such a production was a drop in the bucket of U.S. daily oil consumption.
Realizing that, Congress might never be willing to provide the
huge subsidies that the shale oil firms wanted to protect them
from disaster if world prices for crude oil dropped below the
necessary competitive price level. Oil officials had in mind also
that roasting oil out of shale was an inefficient process, using
more than a third as much energy to heat the shale as the oil
contained. And they were oppressed by fears that improvements
in solar heating or nuclear power could end the energy crisis
before they could pay for their plants.

The same nationwide group of conservationists who had
shown their power in the Echo Park dam fight now went to
Congress against the development of shale oil whether it was
processed by roasting the shale in retorts above ground or by the
untested method of treatment—"in situ"—underground.
Among other complaints, they argued that the enormous mining
activity and its pollution would destroy the celebrated wildlife

1. Sylvia Lewis, "Yes, Virginia, There Is an Oil Shale Industry," *Planning Maga-zine* 40:8–13 (October 1974).

of the Piceance Basin. Meanwhile, in Denver the Colorado Open Space Council was maintaining that the production of a barrel of shale oil left behind a ton of sterile black solid that had to be dumped somewhere. Any considerable production of oil would created dumps covering hundreds of acres each year. Salt leaching from the dumps could contaminate the creeks near them and damage agriculture and municipal water supplies downstream.

The Open Space Council estimated that the projected industry would cause a tripling of the population of the Book Plateau area. Town and county officials would find it impossible to provide the hospitals, schools, sewers, and other facilities needed by a modern community, while the slow-moving state legislature was reaching firm decisions on such controversial issues as severance taxes to give the state some control over the activities of shale oil developers on federal lands. In the view of conservationists, a critical shortage of western-slope water would come with the plants on Piceance Creek and with the hordes of people creating mobile-home ghettos around Rifle and Meeker. The state was far behind already in both state and intrastate water commitments because of the demands on Colorado River made by its hydroelectric power plants—requiring high reservoir levels to operate—to say nothing of the perennial demands of the water-purloining Front Range cities of the Eastern slope. The Colorado Water Conservation Board was warning that at least two hundred thousand extra acre-feet of water annually would be needed for the Book Plateau area if shale oil production met expectations. It could be obtained only by buying water rights from farmers on Colorado River and removing their irrigated fields from food production. Such action was bound to be bitterly opposed in a state that had been based primarily on agriculture since the decline of mining at the turn of the century.

Those who opposed a large Colorado shale oil industry were critical of the coal aspects of Project Independence also, though they recognized that coal-mining was traditional in the state and not merely experimental and short-term as in the case of shale oil. Coal was found in huge quantities everywhere. A popular and cheap method of extracting it was strip-mining—scraping off and pushing aside the thin layer of topsoil to get at the beds of coal beneath. As 1976 began, strip-mining was an expanding enterprise in the Yampa River valley around Oak Creek, Hayden, and Craig, and in the Four Corners region of the southwest below Durango. Yampa valley coal was sold to fuel power-generating plants that supplied electricity to customers in and out of the state. Southwestern coal was sold to two vast power plants on the Navajo Reservation and to two proposed gasification plants in northern New Mexico. The shortage of water was hampering the growth of strip-mining and power generation in both regions, creating demands by the coal operators for still more dams and reservoirs involving White and Yampa rivers in the northwest and branches of the San Juan in the southwest, to be followed by the withdrawal of land that they irrigated from agricultural use. To environmentalists, another paramount issue was the need for laws requiring strip miners to restore the top-soil to its original productive condition after the coal was re-moved.

In contrast to these mining plans to disturb the environment were the measures to preserve it that had been proposed ever since the conservationist pioneering of Theodore Roosevelt and Enos Mills. A principal catalyst in their promotion through the years was a group called the Colorado Mountain Club, the members of which spent their weekends all the year around scrambling over, photographing, mapping, and analyzing every nook and cranny of the fifty-odd peaks rising above fourteen thousand feet and all the other 1,143 summits of the Colorado Rockies above ten thousand feet.

Some comment on this club is in order because of its influ-ence on many aspects of life in today's Colorado, including the elevated status of women. The club was founded in 1912 by four women and three men, and it has adhered ever since to principles established by Julia Holmes on Pikes Peak in 1858 and by Isabella Bird and the Philadelphia lecturer Anna Dickinson, both of whom ascended Longs Peak in 1873—principles emphasizing that whatever men can do, women can do at least as well if not better. One of its members was Dr. Florence Sabin, who became a famous specialist in the cure of tuberculosis and the creator of the state's health code. One club heroine, Mary Cronin, was the first woman (in 1921) to have climbed all of the state's fifty-one peaks over fourteen thousand feet. (The U.S.G.S. keeps finding more; the present total is fifty-three.) Another heroine was Agnes Vaille, who died of freezing in a blizzard on top of Longs Peak on January 12, 1925, after climbing the east face, one of the most difficult ascents in the Rockies even in summer.

As conservationists, members of the club have always maintained with Henry Thoreau that the optimum environment was a blend of wilderness and civilization. To alter an environment drastically for reasons of convenience or greed disrupted the harmonies of nature of which man was a part. The club has contended that by preserving the wilderness, people accepted their relationship to nature's complex organism and their duty to protect it for the general welfare.

The club advocated preservation long before 1920, when a young Forest Service employee in Colorado Arthur H. Carhart persuaded the Department of Agriculture to designate Trappers Lake and its White River environs as a tract to be kept roadless and undeveloped—the first federal application of the idea (roads and development were permitted in national parks). Thereafter, preservation had made little headway until the 1950s when it gained momentum under pressures applied by the Sierra Club and the Wilderness Society during the Echo Park dam controversy. The result was the passage by Congress in 1964 of the National Wilderness Preservation Bill, setting aside in the national forests fifty-four wilderness tracts (no roads or motors permitted) totaling 9.1 million acres, and thirty-four primitive areas (open to limited mining and lumbering) totaling 5.5 million acres.

The preservation bill was backed in Colorado by thirty-five conservation groups working together through the umbrella organization, the Colorado Open Space Council. As recommended by the council, seven wilderness areas had been set aside by January 1976 in Colorado national forests—the Mount Zirkel area along the Continental Divide on the west side of North Park, the Rawah area in Roosevelt National Forest at the eastern edge of North Park, the West Elk area northwest of Gunnison town, the Maroon Bells-Snowmass area above Aspen, the La Garita area above the old silver camp of Creede, the large Weminuche area on the Continental Divide above Pagosa Springs, and the Flat Tops area south of Trappers Lake. In addition, three national forest primitive areas were created—Gore Range-Eagles Nest, Uncompahgre, and Wilson Mountains.

After the end of World War II, Coloradans managed to correct many inequities, which had accumulated through the century as products of the state's ethnic diversity. By January 1976, discrimination exercised by native Americans on immigrants from abroad had vanished. English, Irish and Poles, Swedes, German-Russians, and Jews had fused in the national melting pot. Though the three bands of indigenous Ute Indians in the southwest had lost their vast hunting grounds, they were self-governing and secure on the farms and ranches of their reservations, and their leaders were coping with the dilemmas brought upon them by the encroachment of their white neighbors.

At the start of the new century, the blacks of Colorado, some 150,000 of them in the Front Range cities, were forced no longer to endure the segregation and dreary tasks to which they had been confined for nine decades after 1859. Opportunities for education and worthwhile employment had increased to the point where complete equality seemed likely in another decade.

Meanwhile the Chicanos, those 200,000 descendants of the state's first settlers, had made remarkable progress economically and socially while retaining their distinctive Spanish-Mexican culture. They had achieved representation in all the professions and businesses and their men and women had won high positions in the various state governments.

The women of Colorado could be proud of their accomplishments since that dismal January day in 1876 when the chauvinistic males of the constitutional convention had refused to grant them suffrage. In January 1976, at the opening session of the state legislature, no less than thirteen elected female assemblymen and three female state senators were present in the senate gallery as new stained-glass portraits in two windows were unveiled. One of the portraits memorialized the late Emily Griffith, the Colorado teacher who founded in 1916 Denver's Opportunity School as a division of the city's public school system. This school has continued to offer education at a nominal fee to people of any age who feel a need to learn. The second portrait honored the late Virginia Blue, who became the state's first woman treasurer in the 1960s. Not present at the unveiling but there by proxy was the young Denver lawyer Patricia Nell Schroeder, the first Colorado woman to be elected to the U.S. House of Representatives.

Colorado had its problems in January 1976. Racial tensions remained in spite of some successes in dealing with their causes. There was too much smog around Denver, too much pollution of the rivers, too many people crowding into cities along the Front Range, not enough water to go around. Out on the eastern plains dry-land farmers, who had prospered of late through the use of the new circular sprinkling systems, were worrying about the sinking water table of their underground supplies, called aquifers. Uncertainties about the future of shale oil and strip-mined coal made it hard for towns on the western slope to plan ahead. Completion of public works like the Frying

Pan–Arkansas water diversion project and the second bore of the 8,941-foot Eisenhower Tunnel under Loveland Pass were threatened by skyrocketing costs.

But Coloradans were not dismayed as they faced a new century. They knew that problems had always been around—mining and rail problems, labor troubles, depressions—and these problems had never turned out to be as bad as they had seemed. The challenges of the difficult environment were as stimulating as they had been in gold-rush days. Prospectors were in the hills again dreaming of fortunes as they scratched for strange new metals. Solar heating was discussed everywhere as the hope of the future in a state where the sun shone most of the time. Cloud-seeding to increase rainfall showed some promise to ease the water shortage. One cloud-seeding effort in the San Juans had worked too well. Residents had asked the seeders to desist because the extra snow was causing avalanches and frightening away skiers.

Of one thing Coloradans were sure. They did not want their beautiful land marred without their permission by federally sponsored experiments to solve the nation's energy crisis. And they deplored attempts by out-of-state people to direct the management of federal lands in Colorado without regard for local opinion. Resisting such "foreign" encroachment and minimizing its adverse impact on the land were key problems of the crossroad they had reached.

And still they looked ahead with confidence that their enduring mountains and plains would protect them from the evils of affluence and bestow blessings on them, spiritual and material. And they would keep on hoping, as Coloradans had always hoped, that they could preserve their paradise and prosper by developing its riches too.

Suggestions for Further Reading

My initial step in writing this history was to reread, for background, two books in which I had confidence. The first was *Colorado,* by Percy Stanley Fritz (New York: Prentice-Hall, 1941), which gave me facts as they existed thirty-five years ago, before modern technology brought drastic changes to life in the state. My second background source was *A Colorado History,* written originally in 1966 by Carl Ubbelohde and updated in 1971 by Dr. Ubbelohde in collaboration with Maxine Benson and Duane A. Smith, two of the state's leading historians (Boulder: Pruett Publishing Co., 1972).

My own point of view derives from the love of the region, which my wife and I have acquired during thirty years of wandering through each of the state's sixty-three counties. My impressions have been strengthened by the books of three skilled writers. David Lavender's *One Man's West* (Garden City: Doubleday and Co., 1956) brings out the flavor of the Paradox Valley on the western slope as the author experienced it in growing up there. *The Colorado,* by Frank Waters (New York: Rinehart & Co., 1946) gave me a fresh appreciation of this overworked river and its dominant position in the evolution of the state. Finally, I found in *Centennial,* by James Michener (New York: Random House, 1974) a superb narrative about all the creeping things of the South Platte Valley from its beginnings eons ago up to the ecological and political crossroad that Coloradans face today.

The Northwest country from Steamboat Springs to Brown's Hole and Lodore Canyon is vividly depicted by John Rolfe Burroughs in *Where the Old West Stayed Young* (New York: William Morrow and Co., 1962). Wilson Rockwell presents the Colorado plateau and the valley of the north fork of the Gunnison in *New Frontier* (Denver: Sage Books, 1938) and *Uncompahgre Country* (Denver: Sage Books, 1965). Stephen Payne portrays life in North Park in his autobiographical *Where the Rockies Ride Herd* (Denver: Sage Books, 1965).

195

The story of Middle Park is detailed in *Island of the Rockies,* by Robert C. Black, III (Boulder: Pruett Publishing Co., 1969).

I learned a great deal about those early Coloradans, the Spanish-Americans south of the Arkansas, by reading David Lavender's story of the fur trade, *Bent's Fort* (Garden City: Doubleday and Co., 1954), Barron Beshoar's biography of his grandfather, *Hippocrates in a Red Vest* (Palo Alto, Cal.: American West Publishing Co., 1973), and Ralph C. Taylor's *Colorado South of the Border* (Denver: Sage Books, 1963). The best work on eastern-slope ranching has been done by Maurice Frink, W. Turrentine Jackson, and Agnes Wright Spring in *When Grass Was King* (Boulder: University of Colorado Press, 1956). Hal Borland wrote charming books about his boyhood in the dry-land town of Flagler, including *Country Editor's Boy* (Philadelphia: J. B. Lippincott Co., 1970).

I wrote of Central City on the august authority of Caroline Bancroft and her *Gulch of Gold* (Denver: Sage Books, 1958). I learned of mining in the San Juans from Robert L. Brown's *An Empire of Silver* (Caldwell, Idaho: The Caxton Printers, 1965). The exuberance of Denver was laid out for me by Robert L. Perkin in *The First Hundred Years* (Garden City: Doubleday and Co., 1959) and by the entertaining *Denver!* which Bill Barker wrote with Jackie Lewin (Garden City: Doubleday and Co., 1972). For data on Colorado's mountain railroads and their creators, I stole admiringly from *Rebel of the Rockies*—the story of the Denver and Rio Grande Western Railroad—by Robert G. Athearn (New Haven: Yale University Press, 1962) and from *Rails That Climb*—the Moffat Road—by Edward T. Bollinger (Santa Fe: Rydal Press, 1950).

In sketching the free-silver issue, I had at hand Elmer Ellis's definitive biography, *Henry Moore Teller* (Caldwell, Idaho: The Caxton Printers, 1941). I borrowed also from three other biographies of special excellence: *Horace Tabor,* by Duane A. Smith (Boulder: Colorado Associated University Press, 1973); *William Gilpin* by Thomas L. Karnes (Austin: University of Texas Press, 1970); and *Frontier Capitalist* (John Evans) by Harry E. Kelsey, Jr. (Boulder: Pruett Publishing Co., 1969).

All these books were of tremendous help to me. But my debt is greatest to the hundreds of papers on Colorado subjects contained in the thirty volumes of *The Denver Westerners Brand Book*—labors of love written by members of the Denver Westerners; and to hundreds of other papers published over the past half century in the State Historical Society's quarterly, *The Colorado Magazine*.

Index

Index

Oil shale industry, 185, 186–188, 189–190
Open range. *See* Cattle industry
Open Space Council, 189
Oregon Trail, 13, 14, 18, 22, 34
Ouray, Chief, 84, 86–88, 93, 97–98, 105

Paepcke, Elizabeth, 177–178
Paepcke, Walter, 177, 178, 179–180
Paiutes. *See* Indians: Paiute
Palmer, William J.: railroad builder, 53–54, 56–57, 100; resort builder, 57, 137–139; and Meeker, 60; at statehood day, 75; mentioned, 102, 105, 134, 186
Panics: of 1857, 26; of 1873, 57; of 1893, 103, 112
Pearce, Richard B., 51
Penrose, Spencer, 145–146, 147, 162, 171
Peterson Field, 172
Pike, Zebulon M., 6–8, 14, 137
Pikes Peak: seen by Pike, 6; Frémont at, 18; gold rush to, 26–28; climbed by women, 27, 79; gold on, 115; automobiles on, 142; and Penrose, 145–147; Hill Climb, 146; art academy at, 163, army camp at, 171; mentioned, 44, 54, 80, 137, 174
Pikes Peakers: and Colorado Territory, 29, 30–31, 32; and Indians, 39; at Washington, 170, 173
Pinchot, Gifford, 120, 123, 125–126, 145, 178
Plains Indians, *See* Indians
Plutonium. *See* Minerals
Populist party, 113
Powell, John W., 78–79, 83, 93, 119–120, 182
Prairie Land Company, 69
Project Independence, 185, 189–190
Prospectors: Spanish, 4; and mountain men, 9; in 1859, 28, 86, 194; at Cripple Creek, 116; for uranium, 175–176
Prowers, John Wesley, 68–69, 106
Public Works Administration (PWA), 167
Pueblos. *See* Indians: ancient Anasazi

Race relations: sheepmen and cattlemen, 70; Utes and army, 95–96; effect of KKK, 149; improvement in, 192–193
Railroads: Gilpin's dream of, 16, 32; transcontinental, 47–48, 131; development

of, 52–53; construction of, 56–57; narrow-gauge, 57, 100, 132, 139; fenced right-of-way, 70–71; effect of on science, 85; expansion of, 100; and land development, 107–108; and townsites, 110–111; and tourism, 139; mentioned, 87. *See also* individual railroads by name.
Raton Pass, 4, 9, 21, 35, 67
Resort industry, 55–56, 140, 141, 144, 146–147
Rio Blanco Oil Shale Project, 187, 188
Roche, Josephine: and the UMW, 154, 159
Rocky Mountain Arsenal, 170
Rocky Mountain National Park, 30, 63, 143–145; 169
Roosevelt, Franklin D., 158–159, 169, 182
Roosevelt, Theodore: and conservation, 119–121, 123; becomes president, 125; and forest reserves, 125, 126; mentioned, 158, 190
Routt, John L.: governor, 74, 75

Sand Creek Massacre, 40–41, 42
Santa Fe Trail, 9, 10, 31
Schroeder, Nell: congresswoman, 193
Schwayder, Jesse, 150
Shadow Mountain Reservoir, 169
Shale oil industry. *See* Oil shale industry
Sheep industry, 69–70, 126
Sherman Silver Purchase Act of 1890, 113
Short Line Railroad, 124
Sierra Club, 191
Silver: smelting, 50; at Silverton, 80; at Leadville, 88–89; Little Pittsburg mine, 89, 90; overproduction, 112, 113, 117. *See also* Minerals.
Silver Purchase Act of 1934, 159
Ski industry, 176, 178–179
Soddy, 109
Solar heating, 188, 194
Spanish-Americans. *See* Colorado: ethnic groups
Stanley, Freelan, 142–144
Steamboat Springs, 19, 99, 133, 179
Stewart, Philip B., 121–122, 128
Stratton, Winfield S., 116–117, 124
Strip-mining, 186, 190
Sugar-beet industry, 123–124, 148